# design ideas
# for your garden
inspired by the National Trust

# design ideas for your garden

inspired by the National Trust

Jacq Barber

**National Trust**

*For Mike and Flossy*

First published in the United Kingdom in 2013 by
National Trust Books
10 Southcombe Street
London W14 0RA

An imprint of Anova Books Company Ltd

ISBN 9781907892417

A CIP catalogue record for this book is available from the British Library.

21 20 19 18 17 16 15 14 13
10 9 8 7 6 5 4 3 2 1

Reproduction by Mission Productions Ltd, Hong Kong
Printed and bound by 1010 Printing International Ltd, China

This book can be ordered direct from the publisher at the website www.anovabooks.com, or
try your local bookshop. Also available at National Trust shops and shop.nationaltrust.org.uk.

*Above*: A gardener's trug
in the Garden Hall at
Coughton Court.

*Right:* Outside the potting
shed at Snowshill Manor,
fir cones make a decorative
weather barometer,
closing when wet and
opening up when dry.

*Previous page:* White
foxgloves flowering in
the Rose Garden at
Mottisfont Abbey.

# contents

# introduction

The vast range of garden styles at National Trust properties can provide a rich source of inspiration to anyone thinking of making their own garden. Their original owners were passionate and pioneering, introducing new plants, adopting the very latest fashions and employing the greatest garden designers and generations of expert gardeners. They created some of the most exciting and notable contemporary gardens of their day.

The cherry orchard at Hinton Ampner in spring. Combining the formal and informal, harmony and surprise, the whole garden is full of inspiring ideas for today's gardeners.

Yet it is not just period design that today's National Trust gardeners maintain – they also need the skills to keep things moving forward, in the same spirit in which these gardens were originally created. If you are looking for fresh ideas for your garden, from potagers to planting in pots and stylish borders, this book will point you in the direction of some imaginative design solutions alongside those that have stood the test of time. Chapters on colour, planting styles and ways to create interest throughout the four seasons provide suggestions for keeping your garden looking great all year round. You will also find valuable advice from Head Gardeners and a useful source list of suppliers and organisations for everything you might need to help create the garden you want.

What captivates and inspires us is not always the grand vistas but the unexpected delight found in small details that can be brought into any garden, whatever its size. The photographs in this book illustrate some of the best to be found in National Trust gardens, but by no means all. I hope you will enjoy seeing how some of these ideas might work in your own garden and feel inspired to visit a few of the wonderful places from which they are taken.

Jacq Barber

# planning your garden

# garden elements

**Before you start buying any plants, take a good long look at your garden as your first step towards remaking it. Just as you would when designing a room, consider all the opportunities it presents; even within a small plot you can create an outdoor space as ingenious and diverse as any area inside your home. Think about how you can imprint your own personality and taste on your garden and make it unique to you.**

Keep a scrapbook of ideas, photographs and notes of plant combinations that appeal, as well as clever design solutions for particular sites. If you have enough space, work on creating different themes or areas in your garden, thinking about the flow through the site and how to connect those areas together.

It's easy to become so caught up with planning colour combinations that you forget about the permanent features that are needed to provide the garden with focus and structure. These may consist of hard landscaping such as paving, steps and walls, but they may equally well be structural plants such as clipped evergreens, hedges and topiary – no matter what the scale, they help to hold a garden together.

*Previous page*: At Buscot Park, spectacular pink and white Judas trees (*Cercis siliquastrum* and *C. siliquastrum* 'Alba') make an unusual and spectacular choice of cover for iron arbour tunnels. It provides an enticing walkway, with dappled shade, bright colour and scent in late spring and summer.

*Above*: The garden terraces at Alfriston Clergy House were laid out in the 1920s in an Arts and Crafts design. A formal garden with a central sundial is set in the middle of patterned brick paths leading out to four symmetrical beds, each with clipped golden-edged box trees underplanted with dianthus. This is a good example of how architecture and planting combined can create mood and character.

*Left*: Drawing a plan of your garden is always a good starting point. This sketch by Rudyard Kipling for the planting of the Rose Garden at Bateman's is dated 1906.

# boundaries

*Above*: Through a doorway into the Rose Garden at Sissinghurst Castle, the striking climber *Actinidia kolomikta* can be seen covering the wall. The white and pink splashes on the tips of the leaves look as if they've been dipped in paint.

Most gardens have boundaries of stone, brick, fencing, trellis or hedge. Think of them as design elements in your garden, much like the internal walls of a house, and plan from the boundaries inwards. Living walls such as hedges provide interest all year round, while masonry walls covered with plants look attractive and blur the edges of a garden. Evergreen ivy and climbing hydrangea are good choices for a north-facing wall, while clematis and roses add a splash of spring and summer colour.

*Right*: Growing fruit trees along walls as espaliers is a centuries-old technique that is space-saving if you don't have room for standard trees. Here, an espaliered apple tree is planted against the garden wall at Erddig.

# paths and paving

A wide range of materials can be used for paving and paths, including stone chippings, brick, gravel-topped tarmac, cobbles and grass for paths. Indigenous materials are a good choice, as they will always complement the surrounding landscape and buildings.

The paving in National Trust gardens offers many inspiring ideas from the past. 'Herringbone' is a particularly decorative 'V'-shaped pattern that recurs across centuries and cultures in the design of cloth, parquetry, embroidery, masonry and other materials.

A serpentine path can help to make a garden seem larger. The other appeal of a winding path is its element of intrigue, a sense of anticipation at what might be discovered around the corner. It was a favourite device used in eighteenth-century landscape gardens such as Stourhead.

*Below*: A path winds through the bog garden at Dunham Massey.

*Below:* The sinuous paths in the Terrace Garden at Castle Drogo were designed by the architect Edwin Lutyens in the 1920s and echo an Indian motif on a pergola at the Viceroy's Palace in New Delhi where Lutyens had been working. Plantsman George Dillistone introduced islands of herbaceous planting to complement the structure of Lutyens' paths, using colour, height and texture to great effect.

# get the look

You don't need a huge space to introduce paths that snake from one area to another. A simple figure-of-eight design can make a narrow garden feel wider, provide interestingly shaped borders to fill with plants and extend the time it takes to walk around the garden.

*Above*: Bricks laid out in a herringbone design form the pavement around the Lily Garden at Barrington Court. The pattern was popular among Arts and Crafts designers in the early 1920s.

*Left*: Paving always looks more convincing if it mirrors local materials. In the Old Garden at Hidcote, Lawrence Johnston sliced Cotswold staddle stones to create a style of crazy paving. You can lay crazy paving, using stone, slate or concrete, to create the same pleasingly informal feel.

Hart's tongue fern (*Asplenium scolopendrium*), *Corydalis lutea* and Mind-your-own-business (*Soleirolia soleirolii*) have self-seeded in the shaded crevices of these Cotswolds steps, adding beauty and interest. Often the most charming effects are created by happy accidents.

True to the Arts and Crafts ethos, these beautiful semi-circular Cotswold stone steps are typical of the vernacular materials used throughout the garden at Snowshill Manor. The mock orange, (*Philadelphus* 'Virginal') to the left of the steps, is covered in richly fragrant white flowers in June.

# steps

Edwin Lutyens considered steps a celebration of the changes of levels in a garden – a useful definition to bear in mind. Steps provide an opportunity to unite two areas together and direct you through a space.

Outdoor steps are generally shallower than those indoors, offering an easy descent or climb from one area of the garden to another. They can make a grand architectural statement or be merely functional. Adding planting around them opens up

Mexican fleabane (*Erigeron karvinskianus*), seen here at Sizergh Castle, is a fabulous plant for growing alongside steps and paths or in crevices in walls. It loves sunshine and sharp drainage and its profusely borne delicate daisy flowers are a delightful contrast with hard surfaces. Once established, plants soon self-seed.

The York stone paving and steps at Nunnington Hall are clothed on either side by Lady's mantle (*Alchemilla mollis*) tumbling over and between the treads, providing a softness and delicacy which contrast well with the stone and dark yews to the right.

another dimension, as do steps wide enough for pots and seating. Snowshill Manor offers a good example of how steps can be used as an element of garden design, and the gardens at the property are seen as a series of outdoor rooms. Owner

Charles Paget Wade believed structure and hard landscaping to be more important to a garden than flowers, as they provide a permanent framework and interest all year round.

# seating

Somewhere to sit is essential in most gardens and your choice of seating should enhance the sense of place and draw you to a special spot. Tables and chairs for eating out need a wide, flat surface, while incidental chairs can be placed where they provide a lovely view or a sheltered space to sit.

*Below*: You can create an intimate outdoor dining room such as this area of the White Garden at Sissinghurst. *Wisteria venusta* 'Alba' growing over a pergola creates an attractive, scented and shaded seating area for entertaining, using the wall as a backdrop and shelter.

*Above*: The placing of this wrought iron seat at the end of the lime bower at Hidcote provides a focal point as well as an attractive, sheltered place to sit, offering views over the garden below.

*Above*: Seats don't have to be manmade or formal – sometimes nature obliges. This lovely bench has been made using moss- and lichen-covered stone and blends into a shady box hedge at Plas yn Rhiw. Situated high up in the garden, it provides a spectacular view over Hell's Mouth Bay.

*Above left*: Edwin Lutyens first designed this elegant bench for the garden at Little Thakeham in West Sussex. Its distinctive curved back and arms, like an outdoor sofa, have helped to make it a design classic still reproduced today and it is seen here at William Morris's Red House.

*Left*: At Snowshill Manor, an old wooden bench snuggles cosily into cloud box hedging.

# framing a view

Vistas framed by hedges, archways, double borders, pergolas, doorways, windows and tunnels are some of the most exciting ways to draw the eye into another part of the garden. If you have the room, an avenue of trees or hedges is one of the most dramatic ways to frame a view.

*Left*: Light catches hollyhocks that partly obscure the view through the archway to the sunken parterre at Hanbury Hall.

*Right*: The archway created in the hedge bordering the Pool Garden at Tintinhull frames the view into the kitchen garden beyond.

*Below*: A double avenue of hornbeam, trained as a hedge on stilts, frames the vista to the cedar lawn at Hidcote.

# formal garden design

Some of the earliest gardens recorded were formal in design and it's a style that's been returned to throughout the centuries, from the Renaissance to the Arts and Crafts movement and to gardens today. Characterised by symmetry and order, a formal garden works as well in a tiny courtyard as it does on a grand scale.

"The trick with designing a knot garden is to come up with a pattern and then mark it out on the ground to check everything fits before you start planting."
*Alison Pringle,*
*Head Gardener, Cragside*

*Opposite:* The East Garden at Ham House is designed after a pattern from 1671 when formality was in vogue. The box-hedged compartments are punctuated with cones and filled with clipped santolina and lavender.

*Left:* The design of the Knot Garden at Moseley Old Hall was copied from an original scheme from the 1640s. Knot gardens look particularly effective when viewed from above, where the intricacies of their patterns can be fully appreciated. For this reason they were often designed in courtyards so that they could be admired from the windows of the house.

*Left:* This clever design for a knot garden at Washington Old Hall works by creating a simple but effective 'over and under' pattern with box. The pattern was first marked out with pegs and string, with a weed-suppressing membrane covering well-prepared soil. Small box bushes were planted through slits in the membrane, then gravel was laid between. Although it looks intricate, this is a fairly low-maintenance area of the garden and the box hedges are clipped just once a year.

# topiary

An ancient garden art, topiary is most closely associated with
formal garden design but can be just as effective as a one-off
piece of decoration in a pot. Box and yew are the most common
plants used in topiary for their small leaves and compact
growth, but other evergreens such as holly, Portuguese laurel
*Phillyrea latifolia* and *Lonicera nitida* also work well.

## get the look

The beauty of formal design is that it encapsulates many elements that make a successful garden, such as structure, unity and order. Clipped hedges of yew or box provide an evergreen template all year round and a garden that looks as good in midwinter as it does in high summer.

Topiary shapes can be as simple as a box ball in a pot which can be clipped freehand, but if you feel adventurous, use a framework to create more complex shapes. These can be bought off the shelf or you could try making your own out of wire netting. Place the framework over the plant and tie stems into it, then pinch back new growth to encourage branching out in order to fill any gaps.

*Above*: The topiary mushroom and cone-shaped yews lining the Long Walk at Hinton Ampner make up part of the garden's unique character. Look at topiary as living garden sculpture, a chance to get creative with the shears and produce an individual work of art for your garden.

*Left*: Simple topiary shapes in the garden at West Green House.

"Try using soft, tubular ties for topiary work, as they expand with the plant and do not restrict the flow of sap. Remember to untie any that are too tight to prevent the plant dying back."
**Neil Porteous, Gardens Manager, Mount Stewart**

# planting style

Choosing a planting style for your garden is like putting together a mood board for a room. You need to consider your own taste, the look you want to create, how different elements will work together and how the finished scheme will look.

Gardens grow and change with the seasons, so one of the biggest challenges is to keep colour and interest going throughout the year. A beautiful plant combination may look seductive in a gardening magazine but may only be in flower for three weeks, so succession planting is key.

National Trust gardeners have got this down to a fine art and the borders at Sissinghurst show how to orchestrate subtle changes over a period of several months, keeping the show going from early to late summer. You could try experimenting with some of these plant combinations in your own garden.

*Above left*: The Purple Border at Sissinghurst in early June: bi-coloured lupins (*Lupinus* 'Blue Jacket') flower in the foreground, with bright magenta splashes of the Byzantine gladiolus (*Gladiolus communis* subsp. *byzantinus*) and *Geranium psilostemon*. At the back of the border is a drift of blue *Campanula lactiflora* next to the herbaceous (rather than climbing) *Clematis x durandii* which is just beginning to produce its dark violet blue flowers. Growing over the oak door to the library the vigorous rambling *Rosa* 'Paul Transon' has fragrant, salmon-pink double flowers.

*Above*: The same view in August, and *Aster x frikartii* 'Wunder von Stäfa' is covered in lavender-blue daisy flowers at the front of the border. The butterflies appreciate *Buddleja lindleyana* with its dark violet panicles, and beyond this are the large flower spikes of purple loosestrife (*Lythrum salicaria* 'Robert') and the red hips of *Rosa* 'Geranium' borne on arching stems above the border.

# the outdoor room

Treating garden space as an extension of our home – the 'outdoor room' – is not a modern notion. Its origins date back to the Arts and Crafts movement, with the idea first realised by William Morris at Red House in Bexleyheath, the home built for his family in 1860.

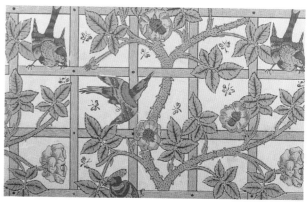

*Above:* Detail from Morris's 'Trellis' wallpaper.

*Left:* Hidcote's garden of rooms has an underlying formal structure. This view through the Fuchsia Garden towards the Bathing Pool is a clever composition. Clipped evergreens provide structure, frame views and anchor the garden together.

*Opposite:* The original garden at Red House provided a chance to experiment with Arts and Crafts ideas about design.

Morris considered the garden inseparable from the house and Philip Webb, his friend, collaborator and architect, even noted plant names on some of the original architectural drawings. At a time when the fashion for ornamental annuals and the contrived patterns of carpet bedding raged, Morris drew inspiration from medieval and Tudor gardens and chose very different plants: old-fashioned flowers such as roses, jasmine, lavender and bergamot surrounded the house walls, and single flowers were favoured over fussy double blooms.  Much was done to protect the trees in the existing orchard while the house was being built. The garden, split into different sections, included a square area enclosed by hedging that was divided into four smaller squares, each surrounded by wattle fencing covered in roses. A romantic, sensuous and intimate garden where art and nature combined, it was the inspiration for many of Morris's designs, including his first wallpaper pattern, 'Trellis' (1862), which depicts birds and dog roses over a trellis. Morris's ideas for division of space and his choice of plants are simple and still appealing, with the formal and informal working together in harmony.

Two of the most influential twentieth-century gardens in England, Hidcote and Sissinghurst, trace their origins back to Red House. However, the remarkable world tour of themed gardens at Biddulph Grange, created from the 1840s by the Victorian plant collector James Bateman and his wife Maria, predates Morris and provides an entirely different take on the genre of garden rooms.

colour

# using colour

**We all respond differently to colour, so the way you use it can make a very personal statement. Colour deserves as much consideration in your garden as you would give to choosing the right shade of paint for your living-room walls.**

The vast range of plants available to gardeners today provides endless opportunities to experiment with combinations and colour schemes. There are three basic approaches you can adopt. Single colour schemes use all the shades from one colour, so a white garden would take advantage of creams, whites, silvers and greys. Harmonious schemes pick up colours that sit next to each other on the colour wheel, for example reds, oranges and yellows. Thirdly, colours that sit opposite each other on the colour wheel such as blue and orange and green and red will produce the most sharply contrasting colour combinations in your garden.

There are no hard and fast rules when it comes to colour but how you combine shades together will produce different effects. You can simply experiment and mix together colours you like or try some tried and tested colour combinations to help you decide what works best.

These bright primary colours of yellow, blue and red work well together as a series of strong contrasts. You can use the illusionary power of colour to make your garden feel bigger – hot colours, for example this *Crocosmia* 'Lucifer' with its brilliant scarlet flowers, advance, while blue tends to recede and white lifts shady areas.

Red

Red-Violet

Red-Orange

Violet

Orange

Blue-Violet

Yellow-Orange

Blue

Yellow

Blue-Green

Yellow-Green

Green

colour wheel

# texture

As a vital element of planting style, texture is inseparable from
colour. At its simplest, texture is about the look and feel of a leaf
or flower and the way it contrasts with its neighbours. Playing
with textures opens up endless opportunities in the garden.

*Above*: In this simple essay in texture, a topiary ball rises above a cloud of love-in-a-mist (*Nigella damascena*) at Westbury Court. The delicate, wispy blue flowers and seedheads contrast in colour and texture with the dark yew ball and the box hedging.

*Left*: The mingled double borders at Packwood in summer play on the textures of architectural plants. Light catches the feathery seedheads of the ornamental grass *Stipa gigantea* which contrast against the solid background of brick and yew. The spiky, silvery thistles of *Cynara cardunculus* (cardoon)and the smaller *Cirsium rivulare* 'Atropurpureum' give strong structural accents as do the vertical purple spires of *Salvia nemorosa* 'Ostfriesland' and the airy stems of *Verbena bonariensis*.

*Above*: This complex composition at Overbecks is as much about texture as colour with its clever layers of contrasting flower and foliage shapes. *Canna iridiflora* at the back provides height and lush green leaves, different in texture, tone and shape from *Persicaria amplexicaulis* with its spikes of fluffy crimson flowers. *Dahlia* 'Fascination', in front, adds a mauve pink, with contrasting purple-bronze foliage.

Textural plants, especially grasses, and those with fine, slender stems, such as *Dierama*, are a great foil against dark backgrounds and help animate a border, as they move and rustle in the breeze. Strongly architectural plants, spiky yuccas, cardoons, acanthus and prickly eryngium (sea holly), with their sharp, dynamic shapes work well placed next to softer textured plants. The most successful planting schemes are those in which colour and texture are used with equal consideration.

# white

White and green is a classic combination; easy on the eye, it obligingly goes with almost everything. White plants are a good choice if you have a shady garden or tend to spend most time in your garden during the evening, as it reflects the light. There is a huge range available, including mock oranges (*Philadelphus*), viburnums, lilies and cosmos – and many white plants are night-scented too, providing an added bonus. For all these reasons a white garden is the ideal spot for al fresco eating in the summer.

*Above*: The White Garden at Sissinghurst was designed by Vita Sackville West and Harold Nicolson in the 1940s with a range of white, silver and grey plants, enclosed by box hedging and surrounded by yew walls. It peaks in late June, when *Rosa mulliganii* cascades over the central arbour with thousands of single white scented blooms, but the real magic is reserved for dusk, when the flowers take on an ethereal glow. Elements of the White Garden can be easily adapted to a small space.

# Planting Ideas

The white form of love-in-a-mist (*Nigella damascena* 'Miss Jekyll Alba') is an easy-to-grow annual which works well planted in informal swathes.

*Rosa* 'Iceberg' is a shrub rose that flowers all summer, seen here in the White Garden. Alternatively, plant 'Climbing Iceberg', which is repeat flowering too.

The hardy *Geranium renardii* has attractive velvety grey-green foliage and lovely white flowers with purple veins.

Sea hollies, with their spiky bracts and stiff stems, are ideal architectural plants for a sunny, well-drained site. The silvery-grey *Eryngium giganteum* gained the common name of 'Miss Willmott's ghost' because the celebrated nineteenth-century plantswoman Ellen Willmott allegedly scattered its seeds in the gardens she visited so surreptitiously that no one realised until the plants appeared.

# red

Red always makes a bold statement, it can make a garden or vista appear shorter and will dominate any soft-coloured planting companions. Red's neighbours on the colour wheel – violet, magenta and orange – have a similar effect and planted together the richness of vibrant colours makes a striking combination. Red contrasts well with bright greens, blues and yellows that have a similar intensity of colour and splashes of red can enliven a planting scheme.

*Left*: The Long Border at Wallington is a rich assembly of reds. Here, *Achillea millefolium* 'Red Velvet' in the foreground is accompanied by *Heuchera* 'Swirling Fantasy' and the paler *H.* 'Pinot Gris', along with the dark red *Astilbe* 'Fanal' and *Monarda didyma* 'Panorama Red Shades'.

*Above*: The Red Borders at Hidcote reach their peak in late summer when many of the tender exotics such as cannas, salvias, fuchsias and lobelias are planted out alongside permanent shrubs and trees, including purple-leaved cherries and *Acer platanoides* 'Crimson King'.

*Left*: Bright scarlet *Lobelia cardinalis* 'Queen Victoria' has reddish-purple leaves, also picked up in the canna which contrast with orange day lilies (*Hemerocallis fulva* 'Kwanso Flore Pleno') and the feathery foliage of *Miscanthus sinensis* 'Gracillimus'.

# blue

There are few truly blue flowers – most range from pale mauve to deep purple. Their elusiveness in nature explains the appeal of pure blue flowers, such as the Himalayan blue poppy with its azure blue petals. While it is a colour that is restful on the eye, too much blue can appear monotonous, so it tends to work best in contrast with other colours. Blue is a good choice for small gardens as it does not fill the space visually in the way that red and other hot colours do.

"Think about the colour of the buildings and hard landscaping around your garden. Grey and ochre-coloured limestone, red brick, slate and granite are very different colours, so choose plants that will work with the background materials you have."
**Mike Calnan, Head of Gardens**

*Left*: The Himalayan blue poppy (*Meconopsis* x *sheldonii* 'Slieve Donard') needs a moist, acid soil to thrive.

*Left*: In the blue border at Great Chalfield Manor in early summer, the herbaceous *Geranium* 'Johnson's Blue' provides mounds of colour at the front of the border, contrasting with the sharp spikes of blue iris and the fleshy foliage of sedums. As the season progresses the border turns from blue into a gentle pink with feathery bronze fennel and flowering sedums. The overall effect is very soft and the pastel colours have been chosen to complement the pale stonework of the house and the paving.

# harmonies

Colours that closely relate to each other combine to produce a harmonious effect, with none competing more than the rest. For example, pink by itself can be harsh or sickly, depending on the tone, but when it is planted in different shades from deep magenta to blush pink the effect is more pleasing. Adding purple or silver to the mix provides a cooler palette.

*Above*: In this harmony of pink in the herbaceous borders at Nymans in June, the silvery stachys in the foreground and pink peony 'Sarah Bernhardt' provide strong vertical contrasts in colour and texture to the bright magenta flowers of *Geranium psilostemon* and the soft pink, cascading climber *Rosa* Polyantha 'Grandiflora'.

*Above*: A late summer planting scheme of flowers which share warm earthy tones. *Helenium* 'Sahin's Early Flowerer', yellow *Inula hookeri* and *Kniphofia* 'Tawny King' are more subtly coloured than most red hot pokers. The varieties in texture and height add to the success of this combination.

*Above*: The double borders at Packwood are a harmony of muted pink, rich purple, deep red and silver. In spring *Allium hollandicum* 'Purple Sensation' dominates and contrasts with the emerging blue-grey foliage of the cardoons and the spiky leaves of *Yucca recurvifolia*. The colours tie in with the rendering on the house, silvered oak windows and lead pipe work.

# contrasts

Some of the most striking effects are achieved when contrasting colours are planted together. Blue and orange work well as each colour intensifies the other, while blue and yellow are a very traditional colour combination. The yellow lifts the blue, adding brightness, and while yellow on its own can look garish, blue tones it down perfectly.

Red and green also sit opposite each other on the colour wheel and make for a great contrast but unless the plants are light in tone, they can look heavy and dark together so you may need to lift the palette with lighter, warm hues.

Colourful annuals such as deep blue cornflowers and vibrant pot marigolds, here with a few stray poppies, provide an informal and effective contrast of colours.

Red and green are contrasting colours and look arresting together. The beautiful rich vermilion flowers of the flame nasturtium (*Tropaeolum speciosum*) makes an eye-catching specimen threaded through dark green yew in summer.

The beauty of strong colour is that you can have fun combining magenta with orange or lime green or adding a splash of brilliant yellow among deep pink with this combination of *Achillea* and *Iberis* (candytuft).

*Left*: The blue and yellow border at Wallington. In summer, blue notes are provided by tall spires of *Delphinium* 'Bluebird', *Nepeta* 'Six Hills Giant', *Geranium pratense* 'Plenum Violaceum' and, tumbling over the arch, *Clematis* 'Prince Charles'. The pale primrose-yellow flowers of giant scabious (*Cephalaria gigantia*) float over the top of the border, while the small spreading *Doronicum orientale* and *Buphthalmum salicifolium* provide a more intense yellow at the front.

## get the look

All of the schemes shown here are easy to adapt and scale down. Try them out yourself or put together your own palette of colours using your favourite plants. Make a note of flowering times to help with succession planting and think about a balance of height, texture and space.

Bringing strongly saturated colours together gives a contemporary look. Jumble up too many bright tones, though, and the impact can be lost in a chaos of colour, so the trick is to choose blocks of two or three bright colours planted next to each other for the best impact. Annuals work well for this and offer opportunities to experiment every year, but there are plenty of perennial plants to choose from too. Playing with colour combinations is an enduring pleasure for gardeners everywhere.

# colour in the garden

**Colour in the garden is now most strongly associated with border design, and particularly the large herbaceous borders created by the artist and gardener Gertrude Jekyll.**

Before the end of the nineteenth century, flowering plants were used very differently to the way we now combine them to create palettes of colour and texture. Plants were originally grown for their individual beauty, practical use or symbolic meaning. From the fifteenth century, they were most frequently planted and admired as single specimens, spaced apart and dotted in parterres and pots. By the eighteenth century island-like beds within lawns, called 'studs' were planted up, alongside serpentine shrubberies and separate flower gardens. When bedding out was all the rage in the mid-nineteenth century, the vibrant colours of tender exotics were massed together for decorative impact.

*Left*: The White Garden at Barrington Court, created in the 1980s but inspired by Gertrude Jekyll's idea of an all-white garden, advocated in her book *Colour in the Flower Garden* – decades before Vita Sackville-West made the White Garden famous at Sissinghurst.

*Opposite*: The magnificent double herbaceous borders at Cliveden were originally created in the 1920s for Lord and Lady Astor. They were redesigned in the early 1970s by Graham Stuart Thomas, a renowned plantsman and the National Trust's first gardens adviser. He was heavily influenced by Gertrude Jekyll's use of colour.

Gertrude Jekyll pioneered a new use of colour and planting style which made her one of the most important gardeners of the twentieth century. Her best-known book, *Colour Schemes for the Flower Garden*, first published in 1919, was one of the most influential gardening books of the century and is still in print.

Miss Jekyll planted her borders in broad drifts of colour, beginning and ending with cooler hues and gradually building to stronger, darker colours at the centre. The main flower border at her home, Munstead Wood, was a huge at 61m (200ft) long and 4.2m (14ft) deep and she had the luxury of generous space in which to create garden areas that peaked at different times of the year. For all of this, her great attention to detail illustrates that her ideas were just as relevant for those of us with very little space of our own. Her style of planting is enduringly familiar, although gardeners have since pushed the boundaries in new directions, using plants and colour in the garden in new and exciting ways.

spring

# spring colour

**The plants that flower in spring are cheerful and uplifting, from soft, pale yellow primroses to the rich Persian carpet hues of wallflowers. Rhododendrons and azaleas, the most showy shrubs of all, are a haze of brilliant colours and clouds of pink and white tree blossom or cascading flowers from spring climbers such as wisteria must be among the most breathtaking sights in any garden, all the more lovely when the air becomes heady with the perfume from so many blooms.**

Magnolias are one of spring's most glamorous beauties. With their huge goblet- or star-shaped flowers, ranging from pure white to deepest purple, some generously covering bare branches before the leaves emerge, they fill the chill spring air with heady scent.

In the Cornish language, 'Trengwainton' means 'homestead of spring' and the garden is spectacular during this season. The brilliant displays of camellias, rhododendrons and magnolias which light up the garden with colour are an inheritance of the great plant-hunting expeditions of the nineteenth and early twentieth centuries.

*Previous page*: The Nuttery at Sissinghurst is carpeted with woodland plants in spring. Trilliums, wood spurge and white bluebells all thrive underneath the grove of Kentish cobnuts.

*Top*: The beautiful upright white flowers of *Magnolia cylindrica*. The garden at Trengwainton has one of the best examples in the country and in April its branches are covered in masses of scented flowers.

*Above: Magnolia campbellii* in full bloom provides wonderful colour in the walled garden at Trengwainton. It is arguably the most spectacular of all the magnolias but you need space for this giant from the Himalayas as it reaches around 18m (59ft) high.

*Left: Magnolia x loebner*i, 'Leonard Messel' is the perfect magnolia for a domestic garden, making an elegant small, rounded tree or large shrub with deep crimson buds opening into pale pink star-shaped flowers.

"Most magnolias respond well to pruning, but heavy pruning may encourage adventurous growth, not wood that will produce flowers. Try to protect the more tender types from situations likely to expose them to cold winds as these may spoil early flowers."
**Ian Wright, Garden Consultant**

# spring bedding with bulbs

Spring bedding in the Long Garden at Cliveden, planted with a striking combination of tulips, the almost black 'Queen of the Night' and pink flowering 'Menton'.

For wow factor, it is hard to beat a well-designed spring bedding scheme packed with colourful bulbs and plants, bedded out in the autumn to flower the following spring. This form of gardening was invented at Cliveden in the mid-nineteenth century by head gardener John Fleming. When Fleming described his experiments in *Spring and Winter Flower Gardening*, published in 1870, Victorian gardeners embraced bedding with a passion.

The most enduring legacy of this form of gardening exists in many municipal parks across the country, but none exceed the scale of the bedding at Cliveden. The main parterre in the garden covers 2.4 ha (6 acres), with sixteen formal beds edged with box hedging and yew topiary. For the spring display, the gardeners plant 12,000 bedding plants and 10,000 bulbs and then change the scheme again for summer. You can use the same plant combinations, just scaled right down.

"To create a formal bedding scheme, make sure the soil is well prepared with lots of organic material. If combining bulbs with other spring bedding, such as forget-me-nots or pansies, don't plant them too densely, otherwise the colour of the underplanting will be swamped – a ratio of 30 per cent bulbs and 70 per cent plants works well. Paler colours work better if you're viewing bedding from a distance."
**Andrew Mudge, Head Gardener, Cliveden**

# get the look

Create bedding schemes to suit the space you have. Choose varieties that flower at the same time for maximum impact. Neatly clipped box hedging works best to define the edges of the beds and contain the planting; dwarf box can be used in smaller spaces.

Tulips are particularly effective because of their upright, elegant flowers and vast range of colours, but hyacinths and narcissi also work well.

*Top*: A narrow border of tulips at Sizergh Castle. The mix of colours gives an informal feel.

*Above*: A minimalist take on bedding-out, created at The Homewood by architect Patrick Gwynne. On the front terrace a grid pattern of formal squares is cut out for bedding plants, echoing the Modernist aesthetic of the rest of house. Scarlet tulip 'Abba' adds splashes of intense colour in spring.

*Left*: At Polesden Lacey, *Tulipa* 'Ollioules' flowers in a narrow box-edged border by the house with the evergreen *Clematis armandii* 'Apple Blossom' scrambling up the wall behind. The soft pinks provide an effective contrast with the yellow-washed walls and green shutters and the vanilla scent from the clematis is an added bonus.

*Above*: The Cherry Garden at Greys Court, with a roof-canopy of arching branches provided by *Prunus* 'Shirotae'. Petals from the flowers fall like confetti over the path.

# blossom

All over Japan, a centuries-old custom called *Hanami* takes place every spring. The word means 'viewing flowers', but the flowers are almost always cherry blossom and each year weather reports are closely monitored so that festivals and parties can be arranged to coincide with the flowering period of a few short weeks.

Cherry blossom may be fleeting but the beauty of these ornamental trees in full bloom is breathtaking in any garden and autumn colour from the turning leaves is an added bonus.

If you have room for only a small tree, just a single ornamental cherry makes a stunning feature and there are many different cultivars and shapes to choose from. Think about underplanting trees, too – erythroniums, aquilegias, bluebells and the forget-me-not like flowers of *Omphalodes cappadocica* are all good choices and provide splashes of colour at ground level which complement the flowers above.

*Above*: The winter-flowering cherry *Prunus* x *subhirtella* 'Autumnalis Rosea' starts to flower in late autumn in mild weather, right through to early spring. It is an ideal tree for a smaller garden.

*Left*: The beautiful double white flowers of *Prunus avium* 'Plena', the wild cherry or Gean.

*Above:* The scheme for the Cottage Garden at Sissinghurst is bold and bright throughout the year with a palette of hot colours.

# spring borders

The borders in a garden start to come to life again in spring as the fresh new growth of herbaceous perennials begins to appear. Early spring is the time to ensure border plants are properly supported to avoid them flopping over and getting damaged by the elements as they grow and flower later in the year. Most National Trust gardeners use pea sticks for this job – coppiced hazel and birch, gathered in winter before the buds burst. A circular 'cage' of woven pea sticks, built around and over the plant with the stems pushed firmly into the ground, provides the sturdiest protection and makes a lovely transitory garden sculpture until it disappears under lush new growth.

Not only are columbines (*Aquilegia vulgaris*) one of the loveliest and easiest flowers you can grow, they flower at the end of the season after most spring bulbs are over and before summer flowers get going. Veterans of the cottage garden, they also look equally at home in more contemporary settings. They readily self-seed around the garden and interbreed, so seedlings are unlikely to look like their parents. Deadheading prevents this but part of the fun is in letting plants happily multiply in your garden.

*Right*: *Aquilegia vulgaris* var. *stellata* 'Nora Barlow'.

*Far right*: *Aquilegia* 'Bluebird'.

*Below:* Spring borders filled with aquilegias in the Pillar Garden at Hidcote provide an informal palette of colours in May and a lovely foil to the formal yew pillars. Aquilegias are left to self-seed but the weaker shades are pulled out, leaving stronger pinks and blues. The Welsh poppies migrated in and the bright yellows and oranges have been kept, adding to the rustic cottage-garden feel.

# a hit of colour

If you like vivid pink, vermilion red and vibrant yellow and your garden has an acid soil, rhododendrons and azaleas are hard to beat for their kaleidoscope of colour in spring.

*Below*: Robert Hyde Greg, was an enthusiastic plantsman and rhododendron breeder who introduced many rhododendrons and azaleas to the gardens at Quarry Bank Mill in the nineteenth century. They still provide brilliant colours in spring.

*Above: Rhododendron* 'Norma' has deep rose pink flowers and good autumn colour.

*Below*: The common *Rhododendron luteum* has deep yellow flowers and is highly scented.

*Above: Rhododendron* 'Daviesii' is a very fragrant azalea with creamy white flowers and a compact low growing habit.

*Above: Rhododendron* 'Homebush' has deep pink, semi-double flowers.

# get the look

Rhododendrons and azaleas will not tolerate a limey soil, but if you have the right growing conditions, their masses of flowers, rich scent, autumn interest and low maintenance requirements make them a good all-round option. *Rhododendron viscosum* (swamp honeysuckle) is richly fragrant and the white flowers are tinged with pink in early summer. Or try R. 'Lionel's Triumph', which has creamy yellow flowers with red splotches at the throat and blooms in May.

"From time to time remove one stem in every three to ground level as this promotes new growth. Avoid the temptation of walking over and sniffing flowers when the ground is wet as this compacts the soil which is detrimental to surface rooters like azaleas."
**Andy Jesson, Head Gardener, Sheffield Park**

# spring climbers

Wisterias are among the most beautiful and versatile twining climbers for the garden. They can be trained to grow over walls and arches and through trees, used as standards or even planted in containers in a small garden. They are good partners for spring-flowering clematis and the foliage still looks attractive after the flowers have gone.

Clematis make a valuable addition at any time of year, trained up walls or left to scramble through other plants. There is a huge range to choose from. The spring-flowering montanas are among the most vigorous and prolifically flowering and will quickly smother anything they can grow into. Another bonus of early-flowering clematis is that they need little pruning.

"Nifty, long loppers are perfect for pruning wisteria. Reduce the long tendrils in July and repeat in January to promote flowering growth."
*Rachel Edwards, Head Gardener, Greys Court*

At Greys Court, a magnificent wisteria arbour created from a mixture of *Wisteria sinensis* (Chinese wisteria) and *W. floribunda* (Japanese wisteria) is a highlight in spring when the long, fragrant racemes of violet-blue flowers come into bloom. Bluebells and aquilegias provide colourful and complementary underplanting.

The moat wall at Sissinghurst is transformed in spring by *Wisteria floribunda* 'Alba' and the perennial wallflower, *Erysimum* 'Bowles's Mauve' which flowers nearly all year long.

In early spring *Clematis armandii* produces pretty star-shaped flowers that have a lovely fragrance. It needs little pruning and is evergreen, so perfect for covering walls and fences.

*Clematis montana* var. *rubens* 'Tetrarose', climbing here above an arched doorway at Sissinghurst, has pink-tinged petals and lovely bronze foliage on new growth.

*Left*: The romantic garden at Scotney Castle with the magnificent white Chinese wisteria (*Wisteria sinensis* 'Alba') flowering over the walls within the Old Castle area. Around an old Venetian well-head is a series of herb beds.

summer

# the flowers of summer

Summer is the season for putting together a paintbox of plants in a border, with shades, shapes and textures that work together to create an exciting composition. It's also the season for the full-blown flowers of roses clambering over walls and pergolas or planted in mixed borders – a well-loved sight in British gardens for centuries.

With the unpredictable British weather, adaptation has become key to good gardening and many National Trust gardens have been planned to take advantage of seemingly hostile conditions and produce spectacular planting effects throughout the summer months.

*Above*: Swatches of bright colours in the garden at Lindisfarne Castle.

*Previous page*: The brilliant colours of Icelandic poppies (*Papaver nudicaule*) in the borders at Felbrigg Hall.

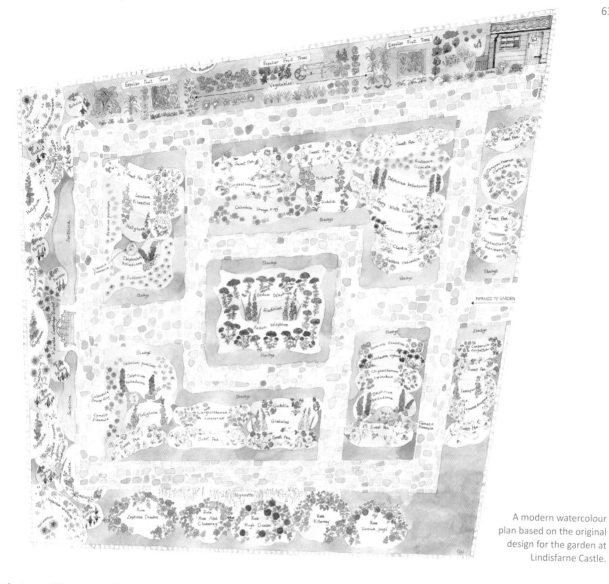

A modern watercolour plan based on the original design for the garden at Lindisfarne Castle.

At the turn of the twentieth century, Lindisfarne Castle was converted into a private house for use as a holiday home by Edward Hudson, the founder of *Country Life* magazine. The architect was Edward Lutyens and, as was often the case, Gertrude Jekyll planned the garden to complement Lutyens' work. There is not a hint of spring or winter planting here; instead, Miss Jekyll included flowering shrubs and roses, vegetables for the house and hardy annuals that would flower prolifically all summer long. Sweet peas, calendula, cornflower, annual chrysanthemum, poppies, larkspur, godietia and reseda, to name just a few, were all planted in large drifts.

The plants here are chosen not just for their appearance but also for their ability to cope with a challenging environment. The walls surrounding the garden serve a practical as well as aesthetic purpose, partially sheltering the garden from salt-laden gales and keeping the sheep out. Lutyens designed the paths and thoughtfully lowered the front wall, so that this jewel box of a garden can be seen clearly from the castle windows, while the view back ties house and garden together. It is an exquisite example of combining beauty and practicality on a small scale.

The long double borders at Nymans.

# flower power

For inspiration on how to create summer displays with flowers, the long double borders at Nymans are hard to beat. This is a piece of lavish horticultural theatre with 6,000 annuals producing a kaleidoscope of intense colour on a grand scale. Blocks of colour are provided by around 40 different cultivars, grown each year on site and planted out in groups of thirty. These are combined with some perennials and are steeply tiered as the borders are quite narrow, the height adding to the drama. Originally laid out in the Edwardian period on the advice of the influential gardener and writer William Robinson, this is a period piece that undergoes subtle changes to the planting every year, ensuring that it never feels static and out of date.

Pink and yellow are never mixed together but beyond that anything goes and the planting is quite spontaneous. The giant topiary crowns halfway down the borders add to the sense of theatre and surrealism, providing visual full stops and a frame for the Italian marble fountain.

The plants are bedded out in May while still small and watered very sparingly in the first few weeks so that they become stocky and resilient. After that they are watered again only if extreme heat becomes a problem. These borders are an essay in sustainable gardening and dispel the myth that this kind of planting needs constant pampering.

# get the look

The great thing about annuals is that their main purpose is to flower quickly so that they set seed for the following year. They are some of the cheapest and easiest plants to grow from seed as well as being extremely versatile. Use annuals on their own to create impact in your garden, to plug gaps in borders, to fill up pots or indeed to sow anywhere you want to inject a splash of summer colour.

> "Annuals give the ideal opportunity to experiment with colour and texture without spending too much money. Take photos of plants you like and mix and match with different colour combinations."
> *Alison Pringle, Head Gardener, Cragside*

The summer borders at Nymans, with dark purple *Petunia multiflora* 'Frenzy Purple' in the foreground and soft pink clary behind. The blue spires of *Salvia farinacea* 'Victoria' and dark foliage of *Perilla nankinensis* contrast with the yellow dahlia 'Sungold', while the tall yellow *Helianthus decapetalus* provides height at the back of the border.

The formal terraced gardens at Cragside are bedded out each summer with a fabulous array of annuals mixed with tender perennials. Elsewhere, seeds are sown directly into the ground in spring or plants are allowed to self-seed. The striking colours of *Convolvulus tricolor* 'Blue Ensign' are combined here with the poached egg plant (*Limnanthes douglasii*).

*Petunia* 'Wonder Wave Purple' is a prolifically flowering half-hardy annual grown from seed. It is combined here with the taller *Ageratum houstonianum* 'Blue Horizon', which works well in borders, and a daisy-flowered *Argyranthemum* 'Snow Storm.'

# herbaceous borders

The classic herbaceous border crammed with perennials and annuals, the colours blending or contrasting with each other to form a mass of exuberant planting, is one of the highlights of the summer garden. Like all forms of gardening, it has evolved over time as new plants are introduced and new ideas develop, and if you struggle to shake off the image of elegant pastel-coloured borders that are immortalised in Edwardian watercolours, a visit to Packwood House will leave you brimming with ideas for plant combinations you will be keen to try at home.

The Terrace borders at Packwood House in June, with the Goliath poppy *Papaver orientale* 'Beauty of Livermere' taking centre stage.

By late summer the Terrace borders at Packwood House have reached their peak.

The Terrace borders zing with rich, hot colours and exciting contrasts of texture and shape. Inspired by the drama of the location, elevated above the main flower garden with Packwood's famous topiary yews, dark and towering, as a backdrop, the border is packed with tender perennials; deep purple salvias and violet-flowered solanum grow next to the bronze and yellows of towering sunflowers (*Helianthus annuus* 'Earth Walker'), rudbeckias and *Dahlia* 'Bishop of Llandaff', with its scarlet flowers and bronze foliage. All are chosen for the richness of their colours and long flowering season.

Other plants are there on architectural merit, giving structure along the border. Plumes of pheasant's tail grass (*Anemanthele lessoniana*) add shimmering, coppery foliage and along with *Euphorbia mellifera* and *Phormium* 'Bronze Baby' provide year-round interest. These are joined in the summer months by the more exotic-looking *Aeonium* 'Zwartkop' and the castor oil plant *Ricinus communis* 'Impala' with its striking deeply lobed leaves and fluffy red blooms. All the tender perennials are dug up before the first frosts, potted up and over-wintered in polytunnels. Other plants, such as verbascums, *Geranium palmatum* and *Verbena bonariensis*, are left to seed through the border.

# cottage-garden style

The quintessential cottage garden, romantic, pretty and informal, is a far cry from the origins of these plots, which were once packed with vegetables, fruit and livestock. Flowers were an optional extra, if they had a practical application. The Victorians, with their nostalgia for a pre-industrial past, were largely responsible for reinventing the more picturesque version we are familiar with today.

*Below*: The land surrounding Hardy's Cottage was used as a builder's yard and for livestock by the author's father, but Hardy replaced this with a romantic, cottage-garden planting style in his later years in an attempt to distance himself from his humble origins.

In two long flower borders at Snowshill Manor, plants tumble and mingle together in ordered chaos, typical of cottage-garden style. Charles Paget Wade preferred soft pastel shades such as sweet rocket (*Hesperis matronalis*), *Iris sibirica*, honesty (*Lunaria annua*) and foxgloves with the odd splashes of colour, from bright red oriental poppies. Wade wasn't a plantsman so there are no rarities at Snowshill Manor, instead this lovely mix of common herbaceous plants could be easily transported into any garden.

You do not need a rural retreat to create a cottage garden — the relaxed, informal style is easily adapted to most locations. Roses and herbaceous perennials such as lupins, larkspur, delphiniums and hollyhocks are among the palette of plants. Foxgloves will happily self-seed in lightly dappled shade. Use honeysuckle and climbing roses and plant cottage-garden annuals such as cornflowers and love-in-a-mist at the front of borders and in between the perennial plants.

*Above*: At Beatrix Potter's home, Hill Top, the borders on each side of the long path are full of informal planting where plants spill casually over onto the paving and colours mingle together.

*Above*: Hollyhocks and lupins are quintessential cottage-garden style plants. Cutting back the flower spikes as soon as they begin to go over encourages a second flush of flowers.

*Above top*: The Long Border at Snowshill Manor.

# exotic gardens

National Trust gardeners have been pushing the boundaries of plant hardiness in an effort to grow more tender species that will tolerate most British winters and add an exotic glamour to our gardens. The South West is home to most of this type of planting, although inner-city gardens can also be an ideal location in which to create your own take on a tropical rainforest. Overbecks has one of the mildest and most sheltered climates in the country. Step inside the garden on a hot summer's day and

you are instantly transported into a steamy jungle or the hot, dry Mediterranean, depending which way you turn. The Banana Garden is the most tropical, where *Musa basjoo* and *Musa sikkimensis*, with red leaf stalks and red splashed leaves, tower above you. The many species of *Hedychium* (ginger lilies) with their butterfly-like blooms are accompanied by the deep red flowers of *Fuchsia boliviana* and the brilliant orange annual *Tithonia rotundifolia* 'Torch' (Mexican sunflower).

*Above*: The towering tree echium (*Echium pininana*) hails from the Canary Islands and with its spectacular spire of blue flowers, reaching 4m (13ft) in height, makes a fabulous addition in more sheltered gardens.

*Above:* Spectacular tree ferns, *Dicksonia antarctica*, growing at Glendurgan. This is the most commonly grown tree fern in the UK, but still needs winter protection in all but the mildest areas.

*Left:* The Banana Garden at Overbecks.

## get the look

If you're lucky enough to have a mild micro climate, exotics will bring a whole different feel to your garden with their large, lush foliage and glamorous flowers. Choose plants to fit your space and growing conditions. Many, such as bananas and tree ferns, need shade, shelter and winter protection, so be prepared to wrap them up warm with fleece and straw.

Cannas are big feature plants at Overbecks, with their lush, tropical-looking foliage and beautiful flower spikes in hot colours. They are left out all year with a protective layer of thick mulch and bark, but over-wintering them in a frost-free environment will guarantee your plants survive. If you do not have the climate for more tender plants, try growing some of the brilliantly coloured, exotic-looking flowers that are hardy, such as *Hemerocallis* and *Crocosmia*.

"Tropical planting is an attitude. It's all about mad huge leaves, spots of searing colour, and a small attempt to mimic natural planting combinations. The trick is not to follow a formal herbaceous style but to take inspiration from the jungle, repeating a few plants in a random manner. In a cold garden combine hostas and ferns and use Impatiens, not bedded out in groups but sprinkled naturalistically throughout, to give a flavour of a tropical rain forest. It's a style, and not limited by climate."
**Cat Saunders, Head Gardener, Overbecks**

# Planting Ideas

*Ensete ventricosum* (Ethiopian banana).

*Canna indica.*

*Hemerocallis* 'Stafford'.

*Strelitzia reginae* (Bird of Paradise) flower.

*Canna iridiflora.*

*Crocosmia* 'Lucifer'.

# gravel gardens

Contemporary, sustainable and inventive, gravel gardens turn the problems of poor soil and lack of rain in dry summers into an asset. Rather than trying to struggle against nature, using precious resources in a losing battle, adapting to change is a far more imaginative way to garden.

The garden at Felbrigg Hall is on free-draining, nutrient-poor, sandy soil, close to the sea and protected by walls. Here the gardeners take full advantage of a choice of plants from the Mediterranean, Australia, New Zealand and South Africa, using this botanical diversity to come up with inspiring and unexpected plant combinations. *Beschorneria yuccoides* produces a fabulous coral-pink flowering spike, while the exotic-looking *Geranium palmatum*, hardier than it appears, provides bright splashes of magenta pink. The tall palms, *Trachycarpus fortunei*, give height and a tropical feel, while the gravel floor glows with colourful mesembryanthemums, gazanias, arctotis, Californian poppies and argyranthemums, all vying with their spiky neighbours for attention. The garden wears its bright colours well, the red Norfolk brick adding to the wonderful vibrancy and luminescence.

*Above*: The Sunken Garden at Packwood House.

*Left*: The tall palms dominate the garden at Felbrigg Hall.

# get the look

If you have an area of your garden that is sunny and sheltered, a gravel garden is a possibility. The area does not have to be large, and a trough-like container will work just as well with plenty of free drainage; the Sunken Garden at Packwood has a 30.5cm (12in) layer of crushed brick over compost. Try some of the colourful South African annuals, such as arctosis, osteospermums, mesembryanthemums, gazanias and other sun-worshippers like scarlet flax (*Linum grandiflorum* 'Rubrum'), seen here with pretty deep pink flowers, growing among *Gazania* 'Kiss Bronze Star'. Contrast with more structural plants, such as the spiky, silvery sea hollies and *Euphorbia myrsinites* with scale-like leaves, trailing here over the front of the border.

"Mesembryanthemums are perfect in gravel against a hot south-facing wall. Their colours are so vibrant it's like sprinkling hundreds and thousands all over the borders! It also adds some light-hearted fun in borders full of architectural foliage and structure."
*Tina Hammond, Head Gardener, Felbrigg Hall*

*Above*: Brightly coloured *Mesembryanthemum* 'Sparkles Mix' planted in the gravel borders at Felbrigg Hall.

# roses

Roses are as evocative of a British summer as strawberries and cream; many rose gardens at National Trust properties were created in the Victorian and Edwardian period when a separate garden room full of roses, often animated by the tinkling sound of water from a fountain, would have been a favourite spot for the ladies of the house.

They remain one of the most popular attractions in National Trust gardens, perhaps because few of us have the space or time to indulge in a rose garden of our own. However, the beauty and scent of roses is hard to resist and with so many good varieties to choose from, it is well worth making room for at least one or two in your garden.

"There are so many wonderful roses to choose from and plenty that are disease-free and require little in the way of pruning. A good mulch in spring with well-rotted manure is hugely beneficial to roses."
*David Stone, Head Gardener, Mottisfont Abbey*

The Rose Garden at Mottisfont Abbey. The creamy pink flowers of *Rosa* 'Adélaïde d'Orléans' smother the wooden arches in June.

The Rose Garden at Nymans.

Old-fashioned roses fell out of favour for much of the twentieth century as new, more showy, repeat-flowering bush roses were introduced. That so many of them survived is largely thanks to the National Trust's first gardens adviser, the late Graham Stuart Thomas. In the early 1970s the walled garden at Mottisfont Abbey became a permanent home for Graham's collection of pre-1900, old-fashioned shrub roses which he had been collecting for almost 40 years, saving many varieties from extinction in the process. This national collection now numbers over 500 varieties and the stylish herbaceous borders that complement them are also his design.

Maud Messel brought her treasured collection of old-fashioned roses to Nymans in the 1920s, after her husband Leonard inherited the property from his father. The rose garden has recently been redesigned and now includes herbaceous geraniums and nepeta, their soft colours and long flowering period complementing the roses and adding extra interest to the garden. David Austin's English roses, bred with the appearance and scent of old roses but with the advantage of disease resistance and repeat flowering, have been added to Maud Messel's collection.

# get the look

There are roses to suit almost every garden situation. For more informal planting, let a rambler scramble through an apple tree. Climbing roses are less vigorous than ramblers and many repeat flower; choose varieties for scent and grow them around doorways and windows, or make a colourful hedge with *Rosa gallica* 'Versicolor' (Rosa mundi). Mix roses in your borders and try training them the Sissinghurst way.

Many people are put off growing roses because of their susceptibility to blackspot and mildew, but modern breeders have developed more disease-resistant varieties. For alternatives to chemicals, spray whole milk on leaves to prevent mildew and use a garlic liquid formulation, now widely available, to stop rust and blackspot. Do this early in the season, as soon as new growth appears, and keep it up regularly.

"Training roses onto hoops or arches by bending the boughs to put them under pressure not only looks good, it forces them to flower more prolifically."
*Alexis Datta, Head Gardener, Sissinghurst*

The deep pink *Rosa* 'Madame Isaac Pereire' trained around a tree, partnered with campanulas.

*Rosa* 'Vanity' in the garden at Sissinghurst, trained over a dome of arched hazel.

# Planting Ideas

*Rosa* 'Souvenir du Docteur Jamain', a deep claret-red climbing rose, , was one of Vita Sackville-West's favourites. Originally introduced in 1865, it was all but forgotten when she discovered an aged plant growing in an old nursery. Vita transplanted it to Sissinghurst where the rose flourished and was successfully propagated.

*Rosa gallica* 'Versicolor' is a very old rose, recorded before 1600. Its bushy, compact habit and distinctive pink-splashed petals make it perfect for a striking informal hedge.

*Rosa* 'Fantin-Latour' is an old-fashioned shrub rose with pink, scented double flowers and is ideal in borders.

*Rosa* 'Tuscany Superb' is an old Gallica rose, with fragrant, deep crimson, velvety flowers. It makes a perfect border rose.

autumn

# autumn trees and shrubs

Autumn's hues are rich, mellow and warm, with oranges, reds and yellows taking on a depth and intensity when the sun is lower in the sky. Along with the changing colours of deciduous trees and shrubs, fruits and berries ripen and some of the most vibrantly coloured flowers come into bloom, leaving summer well and truly in the shade. As it is the most fleeting of all the seasons, grasp the best that autumn has to offer in its few short weeks of loveliness and visit arboretums or gardens with historic tree collections to spot trees and shrubs that perform well in autumn. You will also find inspiration among the dahlia gardens and late summer borders found in many National Trust gardens.

*Above left*: One of the most spectacular shows of autumn colour can be found at Sheffield Park garden, with its ornamental landscape of trees reflected in the lakes. It is a decorative landscape of epic proportions but walk along the lakeside paths and you will spot many trees and shrubs suitable for small gardens.

*Left*: Autumn colours on acer leaves.

*Previous page*: Fallen autumn leaves.

# Planting Ideas

*Acer palmatum* 'Sango-kaku' takes its common name, Coral-bark maple, from the colour of the young branches, which open pinkish-yellow. The leaves are green in summer, turning this deep yellow in autumn.

*Acer palmatum* var. *dissectum* 'Seiryū' has a more upright habit than many Japanese maples and deeply incised leaves. This is one of a collection of maples in the Japanese Garden at Kingston Lacy.

The tulip tree (*Liriodendron tulipifera*) graces many National Trust gardens and makes a great specimen tree if you have space. The common name refers to the tulip-shaped flowers that appear on mature trees, but the fabulous butter-yellow leaves can be enjoyed from the very first autumn.

Acers are hard to beat for the intensity of their autumn colour. The range is vast, from native field maples with leaves that turn a rich yellow in autumn to ornamental Japanese maples (*Acer palmatum*) which are graceful, small and slow-growing. These are ideally suited to smaller plots and can even be grown in large containers, provided you can give them some shade to prevent the delicate leaves from scorching in full sun.

# get the look

As the soil is still warm, autumn is traditionally the best time for planting trees and shrubs to get them established before winter sets in. These are the plants that provide structure and height in a garden, so think about them as key anchors in a composition. If you only have space for one or two trees, look around for those that will provide interest throughout the year, such as flowering cherries and crab apples for their spring blossom and colourful fruits and autumn foliage, or *Sorbus*, *Amelanchier*, some of the *Crataegus* and acers that put on a fiery show of colour at this time of year.

You may not have any space at all for trees or larger shrubs, but there is no need to abandon the idea of autumn colour – you can still introduce it by planting climbers that turn fiery shades.

The structural outline of trees is integral to the design of the garden around The Homewood, with the strong vertical white trunks of birch contrasting with the white concrete horizontal and vertical planes of the house. In September, Japanese maples and the large Norway maple (*Acer platanoides*) start changing colour, reaching a flaming peak by October. They draw the eye along the path into the rest of the garden.

"Select the correct plant for the correct place – avoid buying on impulse or you could end up controlling a tree or shrub to fit a space. Always choose healthy young plants and prepare the soil well before planting."
*Andy Jesson, Head Gardener, Sheffield Park*

An archway in the walled garden at Florence Court is framed by the turning leaves of Virginia creeper (*Parthenocissus quinquefolia*) which catch the low autumn sunshine. This climber will smother large areas of walling.

Crimson glory vine (*Vitis coignetiae*) is a giant ornamental vine with dinner plate-sized leaves that turn a spectacular colour in autumn. It needs space to grow and netting or trellising to cling to, and is a good choice if you have large unsightly areas to cover.

The autumn foliage of *Nyssa sylvatica*, another small, slow-growing deciduous tree with brilliant autumn colour. It grows well in any good loamy soil.

The scarlet-tipped leaves of *Fothergilla monticola*, an acid-loving upright shrub with fragrant white fluffy bottlebrush flowers in spring.

*Enkianthus campanulatus* makes a small tree or large shrub, with pretty bell-shaped flowers in spring and beautiful autumn foliage. *Enkianthus perulatus* is a smaller version with even more spectacular autumn colour.

# autumn flowers

Bold, bright and long-flowering autumn perennials include rudbeckias, Japanese anemones, dahlias and asters, all of which work well in borders or more naturalised settings. Their colours and shapes seem made for an Indian summer and provide colour and interest in the garden right up until the first frosts.

*Below*: The striking sunflower 'Valentine' along the daisy border at Lacock Abbey.

# Planting Ideas

Rudbeckia, with its golden-yellow petals contrasting with deep bluish-brown velvety centres, is a fabulous early autumn perennial.

*Echinacea purpurea* 'Magnus' has larger, more horizontal flowers than other cone flowers and like all echinacea, is very robust and doesn't need staking.

The beautiful white flowers of *Anemone x hybrida* 'Honorine Jobert' will brighten up the semi-shady areas of your garden where it will grow most successfully.

*Anemone hupehensis* var. *japonica* 'Pamina' has lovely deep pink double petals and is more compact and shorter than other varieties, making it perfect for smaller gardens.

# dahlias

Not so long ago dahlias were considered a bit vulgar and garish, but now they are in vogue. They are a flower arranger's dream, providing brilliantly coloured, long-lasting blooms from late summer until the first frosts, and are versatile plants for borders or containers. Natives of Mexico, dahlias were introduced to Europe 200 years ago, reaching the peak of fashion in the mid-nineteenth century. It is easy to see their appeal to Victorian gardeners as they were easily hybridized into myriad colours and forms, producing thousands of new cultivars from the spiky-petalled cactus varieties to the tightly petalled pompom form, reputedly named after the bobble on a French sailor's hat.

*Above*: Lord Fairhaven created a Dahlia Garden at Anglesey Abbey in the 1920s. Around 2,000 dahlias are grown each year from cuttings, with the main Dahlia Garden containing around 80 varieties.

Dahlias are found in many National Trust gardens, adding their vibrant colours to borders such as those at Packwood and Overbecks or providing rows of cutting flowers in kitchen gardens at Arlington Court, Barrington Court and Wimpole Hall, among others. At Cragside, Baddesley Clinton, Biddulph Grange and Anglesey Abbey there are walks and gardens devoted to dahlias.

"To get the best out of dahlias you need to cosset them! Feed regularly and dead-head the flowers to encourage more – and remember to stake and tie in the plants, especially large-flowered varieties, as the rain can cause the plant to collapse if it's not properly supported."
**Paul Walton, Garden Manager, Biddulph Grange**

# get the look

Dahlias are among the easiest and most rewarding flowering plants you can grow. Group similar colours together or contrast brilliant colours such as magenta with flaming orange, or try a range of different varieties as is done at Baddesley Clinton and Cragside. If you do not have much space, choose one of the smaller dahlias which make lovely container plants.

"Try growing dahlias in 3-litre pots and keep them potted when planting them out. The tubers are then intact in the pot when you come to lift them after the first frosts and they can be easily overwintered undisturbed."
**Richard Todd, Head Gardener, Anglesey Abbey**

*Right*: *Dahlia* 'Moonfire' is a dwarf variety with bronze foliage.

*Far right*: *Dahlia* 'Edinburgh' a decorative dahlia with deep maroon petals, tinged with white.

*Dahlia* 'Little William', a pompom type.

*Dahlia* 'Bishop of Llandaff' has lovely dark bronze foliage that contrasts with the scarlet flowers.

*Dahlia* 'Doris Day', a smaller-flowering cactus.

# asters

Planted in attractive drifts of soft pink, lavender blue and white, Michaelmas daisies (asters) are one of the last and loveliest border plants to flower in the garden. In the 1940s Miss Elizabeth Allen became so enchanted by them that she spent the next 50 years establishing the largest collection in Britain. Many of her asters now form a national collection at Upton House, where they are planted in a traditional mixed border with other late-flowering plants, providing welcome drifts of soft colour and structure as well as food for bees and butterflies.

The lilac-pink flowers of *Aster amellus* 'Pink Zenith'.

The aster border at Upton House reaches its peak in early October. *Aster amellus* 'Ultramarine' is one of the earliest to flower along the 66m (216ft) long border.

# get the look

Asters are among the most cheerful of plants with their bright daisy flowers, which can bloom from August until November. Although many forms need staking and plenty of space, popular and reliable varieties such as *Aster x frikartii* 'Monch' have bright, attractive blooms that are very free-flowering and compact, making them ideal for smaller gardens.

"Asters are very versatile and will grow on nearly any type of garden site. They look good in mixed borders, rock gardens, dry sites and even wildflower meadows. They benefit from regular lifting and dividing in the spring; look after them and they will reward you with prolific flowers for decades."
**Heather Aston, Head Gardener, Upton House**

*Above:* The deep purple flowers of *Aster amellus* 'Veilchenkonigin'.

*Below: Aster x frikartii* 'Monch' is long-lasting and brightly coloured – one of the best asters for smaller gardens.

winter

# a season of structural beauty

Less becomes more in the garden during winter. While many plants lie dormant, your eyes are drawn to structure – the tangled branches of trees and shrubs, dark evergreen hedges and topiary. Plants that don't get a second glance when there is so much else to see come into their own, especially under the soft glow of low winter sunlight. Tonal contrasts are greater, the atmosphere is often more still and snow and frost bring their own transient, ethereal beauty to everything they touch.

*Above*: The Winter Garden at Anglesey Abbey. Covered in the white ice crystals of hoarfrost, the plants take on a magical beauty.

*Previous page*: The hornbeam arch under snow at Ham House.

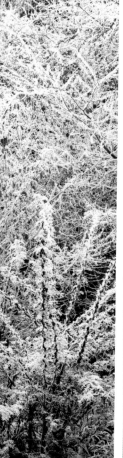

*Below*: *Viburnum x bodnantense* 'Dawn', shown here in February, produces clusters of rosy-pink blooms that are sweetly scented and, best of all, flower all winter long.

*Below right*: The fountain in the Rose Garden at Nymans under snow.

"The Winter Garden offers some of the most exciting opportunities that I've encountered in over 30 years of gardening. Activating all our senses is what winter gardening is all about and the sense of smell is a must to be explored."
**Richard Todd, Head Gardener, Anglesey Abbey**

Winter need not be monochrome. There are fabulous plants that produce their flowers at this time of year, many of them highly scented, and seeming all the more beautiful and welcome when the rest of the garden is comparatively bare. Rather than seeing this as a time for hibernation, create an area in your garden for winter interest and plant some species that will help to lift your spirits on the coldest, darkest days.

When flower borders and beds are empty, the skeleton of a garden becomes the focus of interest. The Rose Garden at Nymans takes on a whole new beauty and enchantment, especially under a carpet of snow. Framed by yew, the arches provide a vista to the fountain, while the snow accentuates the steps around the pool. Compare this image with the same garden in high summer (p.77), when the arches are hidden beneath a canopy of roses.

*Above*: The bare twisted branches of a wisteria at Bodnant become more sculptural when covered in thick frost and catching the low winter light.

Many plants have beautiful seed heads, including alliums, *Verbena bonariensis*, teasels and sedums. Leaving these adds texture and interest to the garden in winter and also provides nutritious food for hungry birds which will scatter seeds as they feed, encouraging the spread of self-seeding plants. Take advantage of low winter sun to highlight or backlight plants.

# get the look

Use this time of year to sit back and take stock. Without the distraction of flowering plants, winter provides the opportunity to look at the overall structure of your garden and see where plants might be added to provide interest. Alongside the trees, shrubs and plants that perform best in winter, enjoy the magical qualities of frost in your garden.

*Above (left and right):* Even simple leaves and the pattern in a wrought iron gate are transformed by frost.

*Below (left and right):* Frost accentuates delicate seed heads in winter.

# planting a winter garden

At Dunham Massey, Anglesey Abbey and more recently Mottisfont Abbey, National Trust gardeners have created gardens designed to be at their best during the winter months. They illustrate how it is possible to have many interesting trees, shrubs and plants that bring a garden to life at this time of year, providing a great source of inspiration whether you have space for your own mini winter walk or only enough for just one or two plants.

*Below:* In this mass of colour along Anglesey Abbey's winter walk, pink-flowering *Viburnum x bodnantense* 'Dawn' is teamed with the evergreen bittersweet *Euonymus fortunei* 'Emerald Gaiety', the yellow flowers of *Hamamelis x intermedia* 'Pallida' and, in the background, the flame-coloured stems of *Cornus sanguinea* 'Midwinter Fire'.

*Right:* The trunk and branches of *Prunus serrula*, the Tibetan cherry, resemble shiny polished mahogany which has just been planed, leaving coils of peeling bark that are golden when backlit by low sun.

# trees for winter

Trees do not just provide important skeletal structure in winter – the texture and colour of their bark can be an added bonus and liven up a winter garden.

*Above:* Acer griseum, the paper bark maple, is a good choice for smaller gardens. The chocolate-brown bark peels away in thin, papery layers, as its common name suggests. Being an acer, this is a good tree for autumn colour too.

*Above:* Betula utilis var. *jacquemontii* (Himalayan birch), chosen for its beautiful chalky-white bark, is planted in groups throughout the winter gardens at Anglesey Abbey and Dunham Massey. If you do not have the space for a group of trees, even a single specimen looks lovely against a dark background.

"To maintain the whiteness of the bark, wash silver birch with water and a soft brush in early December, ideally using a pressure hose – but be careful not to get too close as this risks damaging the bark."
*Richard Todd, Head Gardener, Anglesey Abbey*

# shrubs for winter

Flowering winter shrubs are all the more precious for their scarcity and the excitement of having flowers in the garden at a time when you least expect to see them.

*Cornus sanguinea* 'Winter Beauty', the common dogwood, is grown for its colourful stems, most effective when planted in dense groups. For the best colour, cut a third of the stems back to ground level in early spring.

*Corylus avellana* 'Contorta' (corkscrew hazel) is one of the most sculptural shrubs you can have in the garden, with its twisting stems and attractive catkins which appear on bare branches before they come into leaf.

*Jasminum nudiflorum* (Winter jasmine) trained against a wall at Coleton Fishacre. Although lacking the scent of other jasmines, it flowers through the darkest months and is not fussy about site and soil.

Viburnums are very versatile shrubs and there are many that provide winter blooms and fragrance. *Viburnum farreri* 'Candidissimum' is covered in clusters of pure white, highly scented flowers.

*Daphne bholua* 'Jacqueline Postill' is one of the best scented winter-flowering shrubs and is perfect for a winter border. Plant it where you can appreciate its fragrance.

*Lonicera standishii* (winter honeysuckle) eventually makes a large shrub. Its delicate, fragrant blooms and long flowering season from midwinter onwards make it valuable in the winter garden.

# evergreens

Winter is the season when evergreens come into their own. Their presence is invaluable in winter when they provide shape, form and colour. Their shapes lend structure to National Trust gardens such as Hidcote and Nuffield Place in winter. A simple topiary shape in a pot can work just as well, providing a focal point in the winter garden.

*Above*: Christmas box (*Sarcococca confusa*) is a shrub you wouldn't look at twice, except in winter when it produces tiny, insignificant white flowers which smell gorgeous. Shade-tolerant, slow-growing and undemanding, it can be planted wherever you will most benefit from its fragrance, near the house or along a path.

*Above left:* Providing a permanent structure under a thick dusting of frost, these undulating yews at Nuffield Place could be carved from stone.

*Above*: The snow-covered East Garden at Ham House. Nature provides its own changes in light and colour to an evergreen garden through the seasons.

# berries in winter

Scarlet, orange, yellow, white, black and even purple, berried shrubs and trees are one of winter's delights. These jewel-like fruit are far from purely decorative, providing an important food source for wildlife, particularly during hard winters. So, enjoy their beauty as winter sets in as they may not stay around for long.

Common holly is very versatile, since it can be clipped into topiary or grown as a hedge or specimen tree. Other varieties, such as *Vibernum opulus* make an attractive shrub all year round, with large, fragrant white lace-cap flowers in summer, followed by good autumn colour and attractive jewel-like berries in winter.

*Above: Ilex aquifolium* (common holly). There are many varieties to choose from; if you want berries, make sure you buy a female plant.

*Top left*: The beautiful scarlet berries of *Viburnum opulus* hang like clusters of jewels from bare branches.

*Left*: For something a bit different from the usual shades of red and orange, choose *Callicarpa bodinieri* var. *giraldii* 'Profusion' for its bright violet berries that cling like shiny beads to bare branches in winter.

# hellebores

Hellebores are among late winter's most charming flowers, perfect for cheering up shady areas with their beautiful blooms and architectural foliage. The colours range from almost black to palest white with green, pink and yellow in between, and many have attractive speckled markings on the petals. The flower heads make a great winter cut flower, simply arranged to float in a shallow bowl of water.

Hellebores are a feature in the Dell Garden at Blickling Hall in winter and early spring. The sunken, shady woodland provides perfect growing conditions for over 300 *Helleborus orientalis* hybrids, which flower in a mixture of shades, as well as thousands of spring bulbs planted among other winter-flowering trees and shrubs.

*Above and right*: A range of *Helleborus orientalis* hybrids.

*Above*: The delicate white flowers of snowdrops are one of the first signs that spring is on its way. They look most effective planted in drifts, as they are here in the Winter Garden at Dunham Massey.

*Below left*: *Galanthus* 'Spindlestone Surprise'.

# snowdrops

Passions run high when it comes to snowdrop collecting. There are currently around 260 varieties in the collection at Anglesey Abbey, 20 of them unique to the garden. Although it is one of the largest collections open to the public in the UK, there are some private collectors who have in excess of 500 varieties of snowdrop. Snowdrops are promiscuous plants, with new varieties regularly appearing as a result of cross-fertilisation. The differences are very subtle so it is always a challenge to spot a new one, which goes some way to explaining why galanthophiles (snowdrop aficionados) become competitive about their finds.

# Planting Ideas

A clump of *Narcissus* 'February Gold', one of the most attractive and earliest daffodils to flower. Its small size and bright yellow flowers look fabulous when planted in groups on banks or in wilder areas in any garden.

*Iris reticulata* are among the earliest spring-flowering bulbs and their dwarf habit makes them perfect for containers as well as the front of borders and even between crevices in paving. Drifts of their colourful blue and purple flowers provide splashes of colour throughout the Winter Garden at Dunham Massey.

*Iris reticulata* 'Katharine Hodgkin' has pale blue flowers with striking blue and yellow veining, almost orchid-like in appearance.

*Fritillaria raddeana* is a rare bulb, belonging to the Crown Imperial family, with attractive pale lime green blooms. It can flower as early as February, long before other fritillaries.

# edible planting

# from plot to plate

Not since the 1970s, when Tom and Barbara ditched their suburban lawn in favour of vegetables and chickens in the television sitcom *The Good Life*, has there been such interest in growing our own food as there is today. From allotment plots to container crops, we are discovering that there is nothing more satisfying than eating freshly picked fruit and vegetables we have grown and nurtured ourselves.

*Above:* The walled garden at Arlington Court was almost derelict 15 years ago. Now it is a cornucopia of vegetables, fruit and flowers, all grown without the use of chemicals. Espaliered and cordon-grown local apples are trained over the painted archway, while calendula and nepeta provide colourful edging plants.

*Previous page:* The kitchen garden at Calke Abbey.

The restored kitchen garden at Knightshayes.

Produce for sale, grown in the kitchen garden at Tyntesfield.

Flowers mingle with vegetables in the kitchen garden at Barrington Court.

After decades of disconnection from the land that feeds us, there is a huge resurgence in interest in traditional kitchen gardens. For centuries these productive outdoor larders supplied the households of large country houses and estates with fruit and vegetables throughout the year, but with the decline of these properties after the Second World War, the kitchen garden was often the first thing to go.

A large proportion of the houses given to the National Trust in the late 1940s and 1950s once had vast kitchen gardens with heated greenhouses, hot beds growing exotic produce and espaliered fruit climbing their walls. There was neither the money nor the appetite to restore such costly and labour-intensive sites then and many dilapidated kitchen gardens were grassed over or turned into orchards or visitor car parks.

How times have changed: in little over a decade, almost 30 kitchen gardens have been restored, re-created or designed from scratch. Major restorations at Knightshayes, Chartwell, Tyntesfield, Trengwainton and Packwood have joined those at Tatton Park and Wimpole Hall, while at Rowallane, Clumber Park and Osterley Park, among others, completely new areas for growing edibles have been created. These and many more National Trust kitchen gardens provide a range of inspiring ideas for growing fruit and vegetables on any scale.

# a kitchen garden

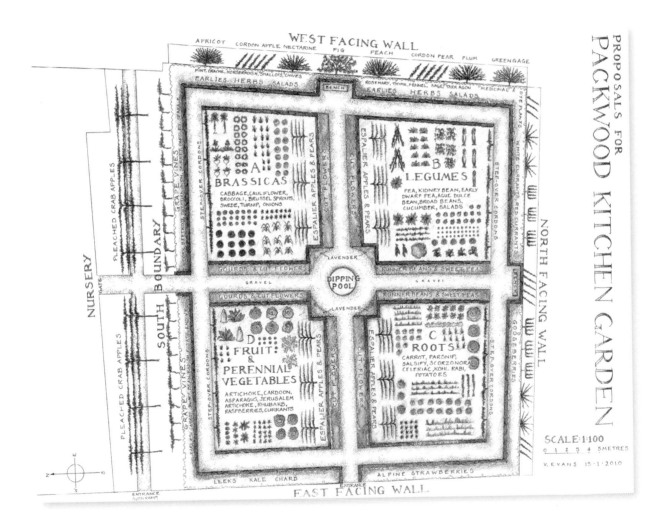

The kitchen garden at Packwood dates back to the eighteenth century but has only recently resumed production. The new design was inspired by a map of the estate dated 1723, showing the walled kitchen garden divided into quarters. The planting reflects what an eighteenth-century gentleman would typically have grown on his estate, with vegetables, herbs and flowers mingled with a few quirky, contemporary details, such as hessian bags planted with yellow and red semi-trailing tomatoes, and a bug house for insects and a pumpkin arch under which you walk with some trepidation.

*Left*: The new design for the kitchen garden at Packwood House. A design need not be as detailed as this, but it illustrates the benefit of working out in advance the arrangement of crops in the space available to you.

*Right*: The bug house at Packwood House, a cosy block of flats for insects made from old clay drainage pipes under a wood and tiled roof. The pipes are filled with corrugated cardboard, cut bamboo canes, straw, fir cones and other natural materials designed to attract nesting insects.

*Below*: Pumpkins grow in the kitchen garden.

# on a smaller scale

The kitchen garden at Greys Court is full of imaginative plant combinations and design details that will give you plenty of ideas for your own edible patch, whether it is a window box or large allotment. Intimate and personal, it reflects the life and interests of Lady Brunner, whose family lived at the property. The colours of the jade-green obelisk corner posts and coral-red edging boards were chosen as reminders of home for her adopted Chinese daughter and the gazebos add a fairground feel, their brightly coloured paintwork complementing the vegetables and flowers.

The entire garden runs on organic principles and in the kitchen garden a wide range of companion planting is practised. Chives are planted around the apple trees to help prevent scab, while foxgloves self-seed in the orchard, reputedly helping fruit to set and keep. Flowering camomile provides an attractive edging to paving slabs and brings in pollinators and its healing properties benefit the health of the surrounding plants. Tomatoes partner asparagus, keeping asparagus beetle at bay; French marigolds deter black fly and nasturtiums are sacrificial plants for cabbage white caterpillars. Sweet peas are grown over obelisks and citrus trees are brought out in the summer, giving an overall potager feel of mingled flowers, herbs and vegetables.

"Mixing vegetables, flowers and herbs together has the benefit of confusing pests with aromatic scent. I love alternating my favourite tomato, 'Sungold', with sunflower 'Jammy Dodger' and planting marigolds and golden celery in front as they are all good companions, attracting the pollinators and repelling aphids."
*Rachel Edwards, Head Gardener, Greys Court*

Lady Brunner liked to promote the work of local artists and Jacqueline Geldart's wood carvings are sited around the garden.

Globe artichokes planted next to purple lettuce, with pot marigolds in the background to bring beneficial insects into the garden.

The lovely kitchen garden at Alfriston Clergy House has eight large raised beds made with oak sleepers and illustrates the variety of different plants you can grow in a relatively small space. The middle four beds follow a four-year crop rotation of potatoes, brassicas, legumes and root vegetables. The far beds against the yew hedge are permanently planted and hold globe artichokes, rhubarb and alpine strawberries. All the beds are underplanted with herbs and flowers including marjoram, mint, fennel, lemon balm, linaria, aquilega, lavender and nasturtiums, which grow among the crops. Flowers are encouraged to draw in pollinators and beneficial insects and to add to the beauty of the garden, which is managed along organic principles.

The potager in the garden at Woolbeding.

# potagers

Originating in France, potagers are ornamental productive gardens where vegetables, herbs and flowers are combined to decorative effect. The most famous example is the vast recreation of a French Renaissance *jardin-potager* at Château de Villandry, but it is a style of gardening that is very adaptable to a plot of any size and has become fashionable today.

The potager in the garden at Woolbeding was designed primarily to be colourful and attractive. A topiary swan sits inside a wooden barrel, cleverly raised a few centimetres from the ground so that it floats in the middle of a sea of lettuce. Alternate colours are planted in ever-decreasing circles around the swan. Dwarf 'Ballerina' apple trees are pruned to provide decorative, compact round 'towers' of blossom and later fruit. Chives line the paths and are cut back hard after flowering to prevent them seeding and to provide a second flush of flowers.

# get the look

Potagers are perfect if you want both edible and decorative plants, especially if you lack space. Most vegetable crops are annuals, so have fun trying different combinations each year and include some ornamental varieties that look as good in borders as in the vegetable patch.

*Above*: Dill flower heads and sweet pea 'Cupani' make a brilliant colour combination.

*Right*: The topiary swan at Woolbeding.

# Planting Ideas

Artichoke 'Purple Globe' looks as attractive in the ornamental garden as it does the vegetable patch.

The purple-veined leaves of Brussels sprout 'Falstaff' make an interesting change from green and the sprouts stay purple-red when cooked, too.

Some vegetables have dramatic colour and form, such as this rainbow chard.

The Italian cabbage cavolo nero is a decorative addition to the edible garden later in the year.

Plant strawberries or try growing an edible soft fruit hedge in order to have decorative blossom followed by fruit.

Blackberry 'Black Satin' is a thornless variety of bramble.

Redcurrant 'Wilson's Long Bunch' bears fruit like clusters of brilliant beads.

# a pop-up vegetable garden

This pop-up vegetable garden is a lively and unexpected addition among the pleasure grounds at Osterley Park. Four plots explode with brightly coloured vegetables and flowers from late summer through to autumn. Dark green kale is mixed with scarlet antirrhinums and fiery coloured zinnias, with gourds and pumpkins planted around the base.

Circles of giant sunflowers partner purple-leaved orach and heirloom peas and beans clamber up traditional pea sticks made from coppiced hazel. In the middle of the plots, acid-yellow painted obelisks provide a sturdy frame for colourful climbers such as morning glory (*Ipomea purpurea*) and Spanish flag (*Ipomoea lobata*).

Everything at Osterley is grown from seeds or cuttings and the obelisks were designed and built in-house. The planting is changed annually – the crop rotation benefits the soil and offers the opportunity to try different plantings.

## get the look

A 'pop-up' garden might look spontaneous but it does require some planning. Once you have your chosen site, take full advantage of hardy annuals which happily self-seed in the garden and will add to the display each year. At Osterley, purple-leaved amaranth, nasturtiums, California poppies, lettuce, rainbow chard and purple orach are encouraged to seed.

> "Get to know your plant seedlings from your weeds and carefully hoe around them – it will save you time and money."
> **Andy Eddy, Head Gardener, Osterley Park**

# convert an existing space

At Rowallane, a small formal area of the garden has been converted from a site for ornamental bedding to herb and salad beds. It is a great example of how you can use existing garden features to create something new and exciting. The four squares of low box hedge and topiary 'drums' provide an ideal structure and enclosures for over 45 different herbs and salads. The spreading branches and flowers of *Magnolia stellata* provide interest early in the season without shading the site. The tallest plants, decorative purple-podded peas and globe artichokes, provide a central focal point around which the herbs and salads are planted.

Think about adapting an existing area in your garden, especially one with ready-made edges up to a path or enclosed low hedging, to grow edible rather than purely ornamental plants.

*Above*: The new herb and salad beds at Rowallane.

*Right*: The pretty flowers of purple-podded peas.

*Left*: The 'pop-up' vegetable garden at Osterley Park.

# herb gardens

Herbs have been used for thousands of years for culinary, medicinal and cosmetic purposes and can be one of the most ornamental, useful and attractive plants in a garden.

Hardwick Hall has one of the largest herb gardens in England. It was created in the 1970s but is a reminder of the significance of herbs to the Elizabethans at the time the Hall was built for Bess, Countess of Shrewsbury, in 1599. Some of the herbs growing in the garden are depicted in panels of embroidery worked by Bess's ladies-in-waiting.

*Above:* The herb garden at Hardwick Hall with drifts of *Hesperis matronalis* (sweet rocket) and cardoons and pyramids of golden hop.

*Above right*: Golden hop planted above a cloud of *Thymus pulegioides* provides a striking contrast of colour and texture.

*Below:* The purple flowering heads of wild leeks planted in front of pyramids of golden hop with pot marigolds growing in the background.

Around 150 herbs are set out in geometric diamonds and triangles with a curved box 'snake' running through to soften the hard edges of the beds. They are split into three categories: culinary, medicinal and others such as woad, which has been used for centuries to make a blue dye. Many of the herbs grown here today would have been familiar to gardeners in the sixteenth century.

## get the look

A sunny spot and poor soil are perfect growing conditions for herbs. Have fun experimenting with the wide range of plants from which to chose; many are hardy perennials and will thrive in most gardens. Plant those you will use frequently near to the house and in window boxes and containers – this is the best way to control mint. There's nothing like the convenience and pleasure of snipping a few fresh leaves for cooking only a few steps away from your kitchen door.

"If you have heavy soil, add some sharp gravel in the planting hole as herbs like free drainage and won't thrive if the soil is waterlogged."
**Ian Hunt, Outdoors Manager, Hardwick Hall**

Borage flowers, perfect for summer Pimms.

Mint is a hugely versatile herb, great used in salads and drinks.

Lemon verbena has the richest lemon scent.

# cut flowers

Growing flowers in the kitchen garden for cutting to provide a regular supply of flowers for the house is a centuries-old tradition. It is a custom that still continues in many National Trust gardens and a designated cutting area, however small, is a good idea in your own garden if you want to grow flowers specifically to harvest. This way they become a crop like any other, rather than depleting your garden borders of their blooms.

At Barrington Court annual flowers are raised in pots and planted in long rows in the kitchen garden. They include cornflowers, cosmos, *Ammi majus*, sunflowers, antirrhinums, dahlias, chrysanthemums and zinnias. This approach works equally well in a smaller border, randomly planted for a more natural effect.

*Above*: Rows of sweet peas growing in the kitchen garden at Arlington Court. Picked regularly, they will provide scented flowers for many weeks.

Cosmos are one of the easiest and most attractive annuals for the cutting garden. Keep cutting flowering annuals to encourage them to produce more blooms.

Sunflowers are a favourite for children to grow and there are many smaller varieties that make beautiful cut flowers.

Sweet William and love-in-a-mist planted in a smaller border.

*Left*: The Wordsworth House scarecrow.

*Below left*: Hand crafted and beautifully written plant labels are an attractive way of marking out different rows of vegetables.

*Bottom left*: Terracotta forcing pots and glass cloches such as these at Woolbeding are both practical and decorative.

# kitchen garden accessories

An edible patch is where you can have the most fun with gardening. Scarecrows give a new meaning to sculpture, while glass cloches and rhubarb forcers are decorative as well as functional. This is, of course, the place to encourage children to eat vegetables: freshly picked and podded peas really do taste like green sweets, edible flowers such as nasturtiums and borage are a novelty and look lovely in salads, and a runner-bean wigwam makes a great den.

The Wordsworth House scarecrow is made of hessian, a material much used in the eighteenth century when this was the Romantic poet's childhood home. The gardeners refer to him as the 'Perchcrow' because he does not scare the birds, which flock to him and pull out his stuffing.

pots and containers

# ways with containers

**Planting in pots, troughs and other containers is gardening scaled down, from a sizeable tree to the tiniest alpine. As long as you provide drainage, virtually any vessel can hold a plant, from old steel drums and footwear to washing tubs and chimney pots. You can either change your planting through the seasons or keep it simple and pick something that looks good year-round.**

Plants in containers are great where space is limited, such as a small paved area, a balcony or even a windowbox. The other delight is their portability; unless they are in heavy containers, you can move them around the garden, sink them into a border to fill a gap and take them with you when you move house.

A plant gets its nutrients and water through roots growing down into the ground, so if you limit it to a pot you need to provide these yourself, especially during the growing season. However, even the laziest gardener can have success by choosing the right plant provided with the right conditions.

*Above*: An array of potted tender plants in the Plant House at Hidcote including spiky *Agave Americana* 'Variegata', aeoniums, orchid and amaryllis. If you have a greenhouse or conservatory, more unusual exotics can provide eye-catching potted plants.

*Previous page*: Spectacular summer container planting at Powis Castle. The pink and red scheme combines *Fuchsia* 'Leverkusen' with *Pelargonium* 'Amethyst', complemented by the purple-veined foliage of *Plectranthus ciliatus*.

*Above left*: Succulents such as this *Echeveria glauca* need little watering. Provide sharp drainage and sunshine and they will thrive in a pot topped off with a layer of grit.

*Above centre*: Amaryllis 'Charisma.' Amaryllis make striking pot plants at any time of the year, flowering six to eight weeks from planting.

*Above right*: Even the simplest of plants can look great in a pot. With their striking foliage, hostas make good pot plants in more shady areas. Here the large glaucus leaves of *Hosta sieboldiana* contrast well with the orange of the terracotta.

*Above*: At Hidcote added interest comes from a collection of potted up scarlet nasturtiums and the ruby-leaved ornamental banana (*Ensete ventricosum* 'Maurelii') which contrast with the decorative lead urn. These pots provide colour at the end of the Red Borders through the seasons and are easily swapped for other plants as the months progress.

# spring pots

A collecting frenzy for rare tulips that raged in Holland in the mid-seventeenth century, known as tulipomania, led to single bulbs exchanging hands for vast sums. Tulips no longer cost a fortune but they remain among the most glamorous and alluring of flowers and are perfectly suited to growing in containers.

*Right*: At Nunnington Hall, the brilliant, deep pink lily-flowered tulip 'China Pink' stands out against the dark yew hedge. The urn is a modern replica of an eighteenth-century design.

*Below*: Pots of tulips displayed in a traditional way inside the Knot Garden at Little Moreton Hall.

# get the look

If you plant tulips in a simple terracotta pot you cannot really go wrong, since terracotta absorbs moisture and provides good insulation. The range of terracotta pots is enormous, from the simple and cheap to expensive, decorative hand-thrown examples. Always wrap precious pots with a protective layer in winter to prevent frost damage.

"We plant our tulips in a peat-free compost mixed with garden compost, and leaf mould provides extra nutrients and good moisture retention. Regular watering maximises flowering time – if the bulbs get too dry, this decreases dramatically."
**Nick Fraser, Head Gardener, Nunnington Hall**

*Below left*: *Tulipa* 'Couleur Cardinal' potted up by the door of the Cottage Garden at Sissinghurst. The vibrant red complements the hot colours of the wallflowers and other plants in this area of the garden in spring.

*Below right*: *Tulipa* 'Texas Flame', above the parterre at Hanbury Hall, is a showy, parrot group tulip.

# auriculas

Auriculas are perfect for the smallest outdoor space. Grow them in little terracotta pots, ideally placed at eye level so that you can admire their painterly flowers and delicate perfume in spring. Stand them on an old shelf or steps or find somewhere sheltered to perch a single pot or more. Auriculas are alpines, so they need to be kept fairly dry in winter and protected from direct sun in summer.

*Below left*: The auricula theatre at Calke Abbey.

*Below*: Auriculas growing in the collections at Greys Court and Tyntesfield.

# plant theatres

Auriculas have been coveted for centuries and their velvety flowers of deep red, bright yellow and even delicate green have a surreal beauty. They were traditionally displayed in auricula theatres and Calke Abbey has the only known example left in this country. It is similar in design to those described by John Claudius Loudon in his gardening books of the Regency period, with layers of staging, a dark background to show off the exquisite flowers and a roof to keep the plants shady and dry.

This easy-to-make, wall-mounted plant theatre at Greys Court is an eye-catching decorative feature and a great idea where space is limited. It holds rows of small terracotta pots filled with violas. Planted up in early spring, they last for around three months with feeds of seaweed, regular dead-heading and watering. Auriculas would work just as well.

Right: The plant theatre at Greys Court.

*Below*: A plan of the plant theatre.

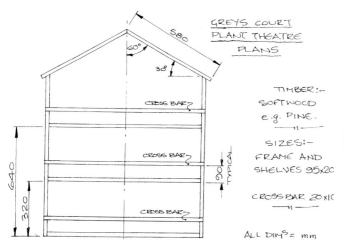

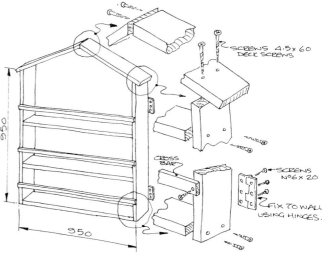

GREYS COURT
PLANT THEATRE
PLANS

580
60°
38°
CROSS BAR
CROSS BAR
90 TYPICAL
640
320
CROSS BAR

TIMBER:-
SOFTWOOD
e.g. PINE.

SIZES:-
FRAME AND
SHELVES 95x20

CROSS BAR 20x10

ALL DIMS = mm

SCREWS 4.5x60
DECK SCREWS

950

CROSS BAR

950

SCREWS
No6 x 20

FIX TO WALL
USING HINGES.

# pots with a difference

Pots can be beautiful objects in their own right, just to leave unplanted as decoration in the garden. There are a huge number of ornamental urns, pots, troughs and containers to be found in National Trust gardens, from elaborate antique pieces to more simple, vernacular items. Auctions, architectural salvage yards, car boot fairs and junk shops are good places to look for old pots and other beautiful vessels.

At Plas Newydd, jars line the top of the wall along the Italian Terrace, adding to the Mediterranean feel in this part of the garden.

The herb garden at Alfriston Clergy House features a collection of antique terracotta amphora collected by the first tenant, Sir Robert Witt, during his travels in Morocco and Crete. This empty vessel has the delicate flowers of blue vervain (*Verbena hastata*) planted around its base, creating a soft contrast with the warm terracotta.

# get the look

Think of containers as garden eye-catchers and ornaments and choose plants to complement the ones you have, planting either in or around them. If your container lacks drainage holes, is too precious to drill into or is the wrong size for the plant you want, consider placing another pot inside it, as they do at Sissinghurst.

Vita Sackville-West and her husband Harold Nicolson had an eye for a good pot, and there are several old ornamental containers in the gardens at Sissinghurst, many brought back from their travels. In spring, the Victorian copper vat in the Cottage Garden is filled with the orange tulip 'Princess Irene', replaced in summer with *Osteospermum* 'Orange Symphony'. Both the rich orange tulips and the bright tangerine petals of the daisies with their violet-blue centres contrast brilliantly with the copper's verdigris patina.

*Above top: Thunbergia alata* 'Alba', the lovely white-flowered Black-eyed Susan, clambers over the edges of this glossy dark Chinese butter urn to wonderful effect. Because the plant is grown inside another pot, it is easily swapped for something else throughout the season.

*Above*: The copper vat planting in spring (left) and summer (right).

# summer containers

Summer is the season when container gardening comes into its own. There are two main approaches to this, the first being to keep things simple and go for one summer-flowering plant. Many tender and hardy perennials work well in this way, such as fuchsias, dahlias and sedums, or plant annuals of the same variety and colour to provide a massed effect, Sissinghurst-style.

The possibilities are wide-ranging and include nasturtiums, pot marigolds, petunias, verbenas or impatiens – the latter one of the few annuals happy in shade. Alternatively, herbs and vegetables are great in pots, including lavender, rosemary, basil, mint, chives, lettuces, tomatoes and chillies, and of course you can enjoy eating them too.

*Below*: Lemon verbena planted in custom-made wooden troughs at Hidcote, designed so they can be easily moved come winter.

*Below*: At Greys Court, an old metal wheelbarrow is planted up with salad mix and nasturtiums .

Agapanthus benefit from being crowded, making them the perfect plants for pots. A whole collection can look fabulous in late summer. Agapanthus originate from South Africa and some are more hardy than others. The evergreen *Agapanthus africanus* at Ickworth are tender and need protection from frost over winter, but they are extremely easy to look after and produce large, elegant globes of blue flowers on long stems.

"The trick with agapanthus is to make sure they get as root-bound as possible without breaking the pot and to thin them down by only a third when you repot them. Water them weekly during the growing season and provide a liquid feed once a month."
***Sean Reid, Head Gardener, Ickworth***

*Above*: A collection of agapanthus on the Orangery steps at Ickworth.

*Right*: An elegant early eighteenth-century urn and the soft pink flowers of sedum on the terrace at Ickworth. The sedum provides foliage from spring before it flowers in summer and makes an ideal container plant.

# grand designs

**Powis Castle is all about grandeur. This is the home of haute-couture container planting, with some of the most sophisticated combinations to be found in the National Trust.**

Every summer, the gardeners rise to the challenge of planting out more than 30 different containers that will keep flowering over four months – a tradition stretching back before 1700, when the garden was first created. In the eighteenth century, the planters were made of lead and held agaves and oranges displayed on the formal terrace. During the nineteenth and early twentieth centuries, many more pots were introduced. Most of these were terracotta, including a Victorian basket-weave design which has been copied and can be found throughout the garden.

*Below*: This fabulous combination sits inside the pedimented niches on the top terrace wall at Powis Castle. *Pelargonium* 'The Boar' is at the back, with double-flowered nasturtium 'Hermine Grashoff' in the centre, *Fuchsia* 'Gartenmeister Bonstedt' and *Pelargonium* 'Blandfordianum' with a trailing habit, feathery foliage and white flowers.

Pelargoniums, often wrongly referred to as geraniums, are among the most cheerful and obliging plants you can put in a pot. With their decorative, long-lasting flowers and attractive, often aromatic, foliage, they will happily flower for months on end with sunshine and a regular feed. The range is vast but species pelargoniums and some of the old fashioned hybrids, such as those shown here, are among the more sophisticated. Over winter them in a frost-free environment with plenty of light and a little water.

Think about summer-flowering pots as outdoor flower arranging, where the art is to achieve the right combination of texture, shape and colour that works with the location you have in mind.

It's easy to over drain pots, wasting valuable water and nutrients, so a drip irrigation system is the more effective form of watering. Alternatively, check your pots daily and don't let them dry out. Or place a stopper at the bottom of the pot to saturate the compost – but remember to remove it to release excess water.

*Far left:* A fiery combination of *Fuchsia* 'Coralle' contrasts with yellow *Oxalis spiralis* subsp. *vulcanicola* and the delicate blue flowers of *Lobelia richardsonii* on the terraces at Powis Castle.

*Above right:* A group of *Pelargonium* 'Scarlet Unique' in terracotta pots add to the Mediterranean feel on the Italian Terrace at Hidcote.

*Right:* *Pelargonium* 'Fair Ellen' has scented leaves and attractive flowers.

# citrus fruit

**Containers have been used for the cultivation of plants since the earliest civilizations, but in Europe this form of gardening reached its peak in the late seventeenth and early eighteenth centuries.**

Orangeries such as those at Dyrham Park, Hanbury Hall and Ham House were built by the rich to house their collections of rare and exotic plants, all grown in pots, designed to stand outside in summer and be brought back inside to over-winter.

*Above:* The interior of the Orangery at Dyrham Park, with containerised evergreen and citrus plants, is one of the earliest greenhouses in the country, dating back to 1701.

*Above left and left:* Citrus produce heavily fragrant flowers all year round but especially in late winter. The fruit takes up to 12 months to ripen, so they often flower and fruit at the same time.

# get the look

Citrus trees look beautiful in pots and this is the only practical way to grow them in the UK. Try lemons or kumquats for your first venture into citrus-growing. Both are easier to grow and you won't miss the sweetness of an orange, that is more likely to taste bitter grown in our colder climate. In winter they need to be kept in a greenhouse, conservatory, or, with some care, a well-glazed porch or sunny, sheltered balcony; they need light and a minimum temperature of 5°C (41°F). The warmer you keep them, the higher the humidity needed to prevent the leaves from dropping. Most citrus can be put outside in a sheltered, sunny position between May and September, when there is no danger of frost.

"If over-wintering citrus plants be careful not to water them too much as their roots are quick to rot. I always add extra drainage to the compost."
**Neil Cook, Head Gardener, Hanbury Hall**

Lemons thrive in a sunny, sheltered environment.

water

# designing with water

**There is nothing more refreshing than the sight and sound of water on a hot summer's day, and its cooling effect is especially valuable in confined spaces. The dark, glassy surface of still water can be contemplative and reflective, while moving water is playful and invigorating, flowing through streams and rills, spilling over rocks or cascading through fountains.**

One of the great things about water is that it does not have to be grand in scale – a simple pool created in a barrel or trough can give just as much pleasure, allowing you to grow some of the wonderful range of aquatic plants and enjoy the wildlife which will benefit from its presence.

*Top*: Sunlight catching water lilies planted in the pool in the Pine Garden at Hidcote.

*Above*: A garden pond is an excellent way to attract wildlife into your garden, including frogs which will keep the slug and snail population down.

*Previous page*: The fountain in the Pond Garden at Lytes Cary Manor.

# water gardens

It is easy to see why water has been a feature in gardens over centuries and in every culture. Incorporated into the gardens created thousands of years ago in ancient Mesopotamia, water was a precious resource to be treasured. Beautiful, formal water gardens existed in ancient Persia and Mogul India, while in Chinese gardens, water and mountains were yin and yang, representing the harmony of nature in a garden. The ancient Egyptians cultivated water lilies in formal pools, and in Japanese meditation gardens, the raking of sand represents flowing water.

Small wonder, then, that water can be found in almost all National Trust gardens, ranging from the grand Georgian water garden of Studley Royal and the rare seventeenth-century Dutch-style water garden at Westbury Court to the theatrical water garden created at Buscot Park by Harold Peto at the beginning of the twentieth century, which harks back in style to the great gardens of Renaissance Italy. Then, of course, there are humbler features such as ponds, bog gardens and streams.

*Top*: Westbury Court garden seen through a dawn mist.

*Above*: The Water Garden at Buscot Park.

# natural water sources

If you are lucky enough to have a natural water source, make use of it. Previously hidden in an underground culvert, the stream at Trengwainton Garden was opened up in the 1920s and meanders for 300m (984ft) through the garden. Along its banks, a profusion of moisture-loving plants flower during spring and summer. Showy candelabra primulas, the deep yellow *Primula helodoxa*, and the purplish-red *P. japonica* are followed by *Mimulus luteus* (monkey flower) with its bright yellow blooms. Soft, feathery astilbes and colourful crocosmia are other companions later in the season. The last section of stream is more shaded and a wide range of ferns florish, including exotic tree ferns which love the mild, damp climate in the National Trust's most westerly garden.

*Above*: The Bog Garden at Great Chalfield Manor was originally designed as a rockery garden in the 1930s and has been newly planted with hostas, ferns and grass species that enjoy the moisture along the banks of the stream.

*Left*: The Stream Garden at Trengwainton Garden.

# get the look

Deep pink flowers of *Primula pulverulenta*.

*Primula vialii*.

The giant leaves of *Gunnera manicata*.

If an area of your garden is damp, rather than go to the expense of draining it, create a bog garden instead. This is done in much the same way as you would make a shallow pond, using a plastic liner, punctured with holes for drainage. It is a good option if you have small children and want to avoid having deep water in your garden.

You don't need a stream to create a similar planting feel. A damp and boggy area can work just as well. Candelabra primulas like their roots cool, so are ideal for these conditions. *Primula helodoxa* and *P. florindae* thrive in marshy areas and stream edges, while *P. japonica*, *P. pulverulenta* and *P. vialii* with its striking pyramid of lilac-pink flowers tipped red will grow in more open situations if the soil is moist.

Astilbes, trilliums, rheums and hostas are essentially woodlanders but will put up with more sun if they have damp roots. If you have plenty of space, try *Filipendula ulmaria*, the native meadowsweet, *Rodgersia* or, for massive impact, *Gunnera manicata*, one of the largest and most spectacular herbaceous plants. If you do not have room, its tiny cousin *Gunnera magellanica* is a mat-forming perennial reaching a height of only about 15cm (6in).

# ponds

Ponds are one of the easiest ways of introducing water and its associated wildlife into your garden, and you can make them as big or small as space and budget will allow. Flexible plastic liners and fibreglass shapes come in a range of sizes and pumps are available to create a fountain or just a trickle, adding that vital element of sound to water and helping to prevent stagnation and the build-up of algae.

You can create a pond in almost any lined container, preferably with a ledge around the perimeter to provide a place for marginal water plants which enjoy shallow water, such as water iris. To avoid hedgehogs and other wildlife being unable to clamber out of the water, always provide a shallow ramp for them to use.

*Left*: The Bird Pond in the garden at Greenway. Japanese water iris (*Iris laevigata*), the giant-leaved *Gunnera tinctoria*, *Persicaria* (pinkweed) with its pale pink bottlebrush flowers and a variety of ferns are among the plants that flourish along the edges of the pond.

*Above*: An eighteenth-century lead water cistern in the kitchen garden at Barrington Court. Cisterns were used for centuries for storing water. Contemporary lead cisterns are available, as well as faux fibreglass ones, making interesting water features in small spaces.

*Left*: The planting around the water's edge in the Rock Garden at Rowallane takes full advantage of moisture-loving herbaceous plants such as ferns, gunneras, hostas, bergenia, *Astilboides*, *Lysimachia* and *Hydrangea paniculata* with its cone-shaped flowers.

*Above*: Water lilies reflected in the Lily Pool at Hidcote. There are varieties suitable for even the smallest pond and their flowers make them an irresistible 'must-have' feature for any still water.

"Planting is the real fun part. Start with large upright plants and move down the layers to the pond and into it. Think about reflections from shrubs or trees – spring and autumn foliage can be stunning when reflected in water. There is such a range of delicious cool herbaceous plants that I would find myself making a pond just for the pleasure of growing these alone!"
**Averil Milligan, Head Gardener, Rowallane**

*Above*: A lead trough along the boundary wall of the kitchen garden at The Courts is an attractive water feature with a working pump. The box hedging in front keeps the brick supports for the trough hidden.

# fountains and water features

The use of elaborate and decorative water features has a long history. By the sixteenth century all manner of ingenious and complex hydraulic devices were being made, including automata, elaborate water jets and metal trees with dripping leaves, such as the weeping willow at Chatsworth House. Fountains became an important feature in formal gardens of the time and their popularity was revived in the nineteenth century, taking full advantage of the technological advances of the Victorian age. Fountains provide a focal point in many National Trust gardens, the sound animating the space and bringing the garden alive.

*Right*: A water wall entitled *Faux Falls* by the sculptor and designer David Harber was commissioned in 2007 by the present Lord Farringdon at Buscot Park. It is made from a series of stainless steel panels over which water is pumped, aligned to appear as a single cascading stream fed from a statue of Aphrodite in the garden.

*Left*: This magnificent nineteenth century fountain with multiple jets of soaring water is at the centre of the sunken Italian Garden at Belton House.

## get the look

There is a huge range of decorative fountains, spouts, water features and sculpture to choose from for your own garden. Whether they are antique pieces, modern reproductions or contemporary art, they can all provide a focal point and accentuate water's qualities of light, movement and sound. If you only have room for a small water feature, a simple pump attached to a wall-mounted spout is a good option and works well in an enclosed space.

*Above left*: The distinctive bronze lion's head water spout that feeds the rill and pool on the Italianate Terrace Garden at Plas Newydd.

*Above right*: The bronze wall mask and spout in the terrace wall of the Armillary Court at Snowshill makes an attractive water feature, especially when covered in the pretty ivy-leaved toadflax (*Cymbalaria muralis*).

# reflections

Reflective pools have a long pedigree in the history of garden-making. While still lakes have fantastic reflective qualities, water does not need to be deep – a dark-bottomed surface with just a few centimetres of still water provides the same effect. Think creatively and use the reflective qualities that water provides in order to bring another dimension into your garden, just as you would place a mirror in your home.

At The Homewood, Patrick Gwynne used the reflective qualities of water as the perfect aesthetic complement to the long horizontal windows and slender vertical columns of the house. He created a series of ponds from the stream that flows through the garden right up to this oval pool by the house itself, cleverly exploiting reflections of light inside and outside. The pool is lined with turquoise mosaic tiles which echo the colour of a Murano-style glass chandelier on the landing of the staircase overlooking the pool. On a sunny day, the ripples from a small fountain in the centre of the pool reflect onto the ceiling of the study.

*Above*: Water is used throughout the garden at Woolbeding. A colourful pot of tulips and pansies is placed to take advantage of the reflections provided by the swimming pool.

*Left, top and bottom*: Reflections in the water indoors and outdoors at The Homewood.

*Opposite*: The lake at Lyme Park.

wild

# back to nature

**A return to nature has been a recurring theme in garden design; through the centuries, the pendulum of fashion has regularly swung between formality and a desire to embrace elements of our natural landscape.**

*Above:* In the orchard at Erddig, late-flowering *Narcissus poeticus* var. *recurvus* is planted in drifts among the long grass under the apple trees. The grass is studded with flowers at other times of the year, from snowdrops to autumn crocus. More formal cones of yew punctuate the informal scene.

*Previous page:* A wild flower patch in the kitchen garden at Tyntesfield.

In recent years, concerns over the loss of natural habitats and the impact of that on native flora and fauna have coincided with a trend towards a more natural style of planting. Domestic gardens make up a quarter of the land in our towns and cities alone, so even the smallest patch has the potential to make a difference to the local wildlife population.

You do not need a huge expanse of land to go wild in your garden – it is easy to be wildlife-friendly in a small space and it takes less effort than you might think. Nor does a wildlife garden equate to an unruly mess, since it is what you plant and how you manage your plot that makes all the difference.

> "The most important tip for making any wildlife garden is to enjoy it and let it develop. As you discover more by observing, you will get even more out of it."
> **Ned Price, Head Gardener, The Weir**

# a wild past

Medieval flowery meads – areas of grass studded with flowers – were among the first examples of the desire to create an idealised wild garden. Later, in the seventeenth century, a more cultivated wilderness, or *bosquet*, was fashionable. This was an area within a formal garden with hedges and trees enclosing 'quarters' planted with the feel of shady, bosky groves and designed as places to wander and sit.

*Below:* The Wilderness at Hanbury Hall, originally designed by George London in 1700, includes beech-hedged enclosed 'quarters' or divided spaces, planted with small trees providing semi-shaded secluded walks and a central area with junipers in ornate pots of the period.

The eighteenth-century landscape movement in Britain, led by Lancelot 'Capability' Brown, turned nature into an art form to create the perfect (man-made) landscape. 'Wild' gardening took the shape of wilderness walks such as those at Croome and Prior Park with shelter belts of wooded areas bordered by shrubberies, often with wild flowers naturalised along their length. Towards the end of the century, however, the mood had turned more romantic and rugged, favouring a wilder landscape in what was known as the Picturesque style.

Some 70 years later, the gardener and writer William Robinson first articulated our modern sense of wild gardening in his influential book *The Wild Garden*, published in 1870. Robinson railed against High Victorian bedding-out with its hothouse-grown annuals. He was an early ecologist, understanding the importance of trees, green space and meadows, and used native flowers and hardy perennials in more natural drifts in the garden.

# the natural style in spring

Drifts of naturalised bulbs and wild flowers are one of spring's loveliest sights. At gardens like The Weir, the year gets off to a colourful start with snowdrops and crocus, followed by narcissi, scilla and chionodoxa, alongside violets and primroses which all punctuate the grassland with their flowers.

Leaving primroses to self-seed will encourage rogue colours, such as pink and white, to emerge.

In spring the beautiful 'wilderness' at Antony is carpeted with wild garlic, bluebells and red campion, with a froth of Queen Anne's lace (*Daucus carota*) further back. It provides a seamless transition from the more formal garden to the wilder woodland beyond.

The garden at Cotehele in mid March with the spectacular sight of thousands of daffodils turning the meadow into a sea of yellow and white flowers, moving like a wave when the wind blows. Most of us probably think of daffodils as big and blowsy but our native *Narcissus pseudonarcissus*, along with many of the original varieties, are small, pale, delicate beauties perfect for naturalising in long grass.

# get the look

If you have a patch of lawn, naturalised bulbs in grass are a great way to introduce early spring colour in a more informal way than planting in beds or pots. By choosing the right species you can have flowers from January onwards, with early snowdrops and crocus through until late-flowering narcissus such as the heavily scented *Narcissus poeticus* var. *recurvus* (pheasant's-eye narcissus) which is also the last to flower, in May. Resist the temptation to get out the mower and leave the foliage to die down so that flowering will improve each year.

Daffodils look best planted in big drifts, but you can scale them down for a smaller garden. Gently throw out handfuls of bulbs onto the grass and aim to plant them where they land – you may have to space out a few, but the look will be far more natural than if you try to arrange them.

*Above*: At Lacock Abbey large areas of meadow and woodland become a purple and violet-blue carpet in late February with the flowers of thousands of *Crocus vernus*. The grass is not cut until after the crocus have self-seeded in order to encourage them to spread.

*Top*: Pheasant's-eye narcissus.

# orchards

Sixty per cent of our traditional fruit orchards have vanished since the 1950s, and with them a wealth of old apple varieties distinct to each region. Plant an apple tree of a variety local to your area and you will be putting a little bit of that heritage back.

The lovely old cider orchards at Barrington Court date back to the nineteenth century. Planted with a mixture of dessert, culinary and cider apples, these include old varieties with wonderful names such as Brown Snout, Hoary Morning and Slack ma Girdle.

Pink-tinged apple blossom with frothy white cow parsley creates a romantic wild garden in late spring. The cow parsley is prevented from seeding so that other wild flowers such as Queen Anne's lace, common spotted orchid, cranesbill and cuckoo flower can get a look in.

The grass is left until mid July and once mown, the cuttings are removed to keep soil fertility down and encourage more flowers. Yellow rattle (*Rhinanthus minor*), an attractive flowering annual which weakens vigorous grass growth, is also sown to encourage wildflowers. In this environment, wildlife thrives.

*Above left*: The orchard at Barrington Court.

*Above*: Cow parsley flowering in the orchard.

# get the look

An orchard simply means a place where fruit trees are grown, and you don't need acres to create your own. It is worth investing in a bit of planning and research, and there is a wealth of information out there to help you. Fruit trees need sunshine and local varieties will be best suited to your soil type and climate. Most fruit trees are grown on root stocks which determine their eventual size and cropping potential, so look for smaller trees if space is a premium.

*Below*: A mown path through the orchard at Hidcote with cow parsley and red campion flowering in early summer. The grass is left long until late summer, as well as saving on fuel and maintenance, this enhances the habitat for wildlife and looks beautiful.

*Far right*: Red campion.

Create a romantic feel in an orchard by underplanting trees with spring bulbs – all those suitable for naturalising in grass will work well. Sow wild-flower seed, in a mix suited to your soil type, in the autumn or early spring for a second flush of flowers in summer. Resist cutting the grass until late summer or autumn to give flowers the chance to self-seed and remember to remove grass cuttings afterwards.

*Above*: Apple blossom in the orchard at Cotehele.

*Top left*: The little apple orchard in the middle of Fenton House garden shows what can be achieved in a limited space within a town garden. Underplanted in spring with small flowered bulbs, by summer the silvery seed heads of grasses catch the wind and sunlight bringing a lovely informal feel to the garden.

# the summer meadow

Traditional hay meadows, rich in wild flowers, were established across Britain's countryside for over a thousand years and flourished in the seasonal cycle of grazing and cutting grass to make hay. Huge changes in farming and land development have led to the disappearance of 98 per cent of them in the last 60 years. Not only have native grassland flora been lost but also the wildlife species dependent on meadows for their survival.

A small wild-flower meadow in your garden is the perfect way to grow some of these grassland flowers that have disappeared from our countryside. Annual plants are usually the first to colonize, flowering within weeks of planting, while indigenous perennials should begin to flower in their second year.

*Right*: A mown path through summer meadow grasses, with drifts of ox-eye daises, creates a wild feel at the edge of the apple orchard at Greys Court. Scabious, poppies and other wild flowers have also established themselves.

*Below left and right*: A small patch of annual cornfield flowers. Bright red poppies mingle with ox-eye daisies and cornflowers, with splashes of magenta corn cockle.

*Left*: This small garden at Coleridge Cottage has been designed to capture the spirit of the time when the poet lived here in 1796. A mixture of summer wildflowers and meandering grass paths lead to a lime tree and bower, both alluding to the Romantic nature of Coleridge's poetry.

Most wild flowers flourish best on impoverished soil and once established a wild-flower patch takes care of itself, with no need for you to water or feed it. You can easily create small squares of meadow within or at the end of an existing lawn; the contrast between the formal and informal is hugely striking and effective. Even if you can only spare a small patch of soil, it is worth growing some wild flowers for your own pleasure and the benefit of local wildlife.

There are specialist companies that sell wild-flower seed mixes, plug plants and meadow turf.

"Just a couple of square feet is enough to create a small wildflower meadow in your garden and you'll be rewarded with a blanket of flowers in a few short months with the added satisfaction of watching the wildlife flocking to enjoy them too."
**Robin Andrews, Head Gardener, Dunster Castle**

# gardening for wildlife

If you do not have the inclination to grow native plants, you can still help the local wildlife population by growing nectar-rich garden flowers. Many modern cultivated plants have been bred for longer flowering but are sterile or produce little nectar. Beneficial insects such as ladybirds, hoverflies and bees will suppress the aphid population and pollinate flowers, so it makes ecological sense to choose plants that attract them.

*Below*: Among the Regency-style flower beds at Osterley Park is this pretty combination of red and white valerian, sweet rocket (*Hesperis matronalis*) and purple toadflax (*Linaria purpurea* 'Canon Went') – all plants that provide food for insects.

*Above*: A peacock butterfly on an *Inula* flower.

# Planting Ideas

Look after the wildlife in your garden all year round by choosing the right garden plants, which generally means seeking out older varieties. Grow climbing plants such as honeysuckle and ivy up fences and trellis around the boundaries of your garden. Ivy blossom is a favourite of autumn butterflies such as the red admiral and the black winter berries provide food for birds. If you have the space, plant a hedge – mixed species are best but as an alternative choose berry-producing yew or holly. The flowers of spring bulbs, alongside primulas, aubretia, sweet rocket, sweet Willliam and bugle, will keep emerging insects in food.

Herbs are wildlife favourites. Try planting hyssop, lavender, marjoram and thyme; all look beautiful in the garden and butterflies and bees love them. Herbaceous perennials such as echinops, echinacea, *Verbena bonariensis*, asters and *Sedum spectabile* all attract butterflies and bees – but avoid *Sedum Autumn Joy*, which is sterile.

> "You can easily grow the right plant in the wrong place, and fail to attract the desired butterflies. Sunlight and shelter from wind are essential. Butterfly borders need to be south-facing and sheltered."
> **Matthew Oates,**
> **National Trust Nature and Wildlife Experience Adviser**

*Left: Buddleja davidii* is famed above all other garden plants for attracting butterflies. It is a fast-growing and undemanding shrub.

*Above, centre and bottom*: Scabious are among the most attractive summer flowers you can grow and all are magnets for bees and butterflies. Alongside the many blue varieties, if you have space try the giant scabious *Cephalaria gigantea*, with 1.8m (6ft) tall willowy stems carrying primrose-yellow flowers, or the daintier and smaller *Knautia macedonica*, which has long-flowering crimson flowers.

# prairie planting

The natural style of gardening which has dominated modern garden design over the past decade or more is characterised by relaxed but, in reality, very sophisticated arrangements of tall perennials and grasses. Its most famous exponent is Dutch garden designer Piet Oudolf and it is a style where structure, texture and movement are prioritized over colour.

The American troops stationed at Saltram during the Second World War provide the historical link behind the creation of this border which uses plants and grasses native to the American prairie. *Echinacea* (cone flower) is mixed with delicate *Gaura* and mauve-flowered *Liatris spicata*. Splashes of stronger colour are provided by the bright cerise *Monarda didyma* 'Pink Supreme' and tall yellow-flowering *Helianthus salicifolius* (willow-leaved sunflower) and *Solidago* (goldenrod). The area contrasts with the British native flowers planted on the opposite side of the path and flowers from late summer, after the native flowers are over, through until November.

*Left and above right*: The prairie planting at Saltram.

*Left: Monarda* 'Cambridge Scarlet.' Bergamot is a signature plant within prairie style borders. It has aromatic foliage and is beloved by bees and butterflies and, as with all prairie planting, the stiff stems are left to provide structure all winter long.

"Experimentation is the key to this kind of planting. In smaller areas, choose shorter plants such as echinacea and liatris, plant them in groups and leave all the seed heads for the birds to enjoy. They will also provide texture and interest during winter when the plants are dormant."
***Penny Hammond, Head Gardener, Saltram***

# new perennial

Inspired by Piet Oudolf's natural style of planting, often referred to as the 'New Perennial' movement, this design at Wimpole Hall brings a fresh, contemporary feel into the walled garden. A variety of perennials, chosen for their contrast in texture and height, have been carefully selected and planted in long parallel rows. Pattern comes from subtle changes in colour, form and the way plants flow and move together. The design makes a really bold statement, bringing a 'wow factor' into this area of the garden. You need space and depth to pull off this kind of planting but the scheme itself is reasonably easy to arrange. Elegant simplicity is created by choosing cleverly contrasting plants that work together as a whole.

The majestic white globes of *Allium stipitatum* 'Mount Everest', dominate the planting in June. *Phlomis russeliana*, with whorls of hooded, lemon yellow flowers on tall stems, are combined with the honey-scented spurge, *Euphorbia stygiana* and ornamental grasses which flower later in the season.

*Left*: On a sunny day in September, light catches the feathery golden plumes of *Stipa gigantea*, casting patterns on the path surface below. Rows of *Heuchera* 'Chocolate Ruffles' bring soft textured dark maroon foliage to the palette and contrast with the taller spiky, blue-tinged flowers of globe thistles (*Echinops ritro* L.). Ornamental cherries, (*Prunus avium* 'Plena') provide height and shade above.

*Left*: The long border features plants with a long flowering season paired with others chosen for their colour, texture and shape. In August, coppery orange *Helenium* 'Moerheim Beauty', pale lilac flowered *Verbena rigida* f. *lilacina* 'Polaris' and dark purple flower spikes of the hardy *Salvia nemorosa* 'Caradonna' make a striking combination and contrast with *Allium sphaerocephalon* with its upright purple tufted flowers and the sparkler-like seedheads of *Allium schubertii*. Threaded in between are the fine, tall rigid stems of *Verbena bonariensis*. Many of these varieties are loved by insects, so attract pollinators as well as looking stunning.

The planting is complemented by the neighbouring long border, created against a south-facing wall, where plants are cleverly mingled together, playing on colour and texture in a very contemporary way. These plant combinations can easily be transported into smaller gardens and regularly inspire visitors to Wimpole to try out what they've seen at home.

map of national trust gardens in the uk

# useful suppliers

## Plants

### National Trust

The majority of National Trust garden properties have plant sales and where possible these feature plants that can be seen in the garden.

*National Trust has a peat-free policy across all its gardens and plants sold at National Trust plant centres are grown in peat-free compost.*
www.nationaltrust.org.uk

### RHS plant finder

*An essential gardening annual which lists more than 70,000 plants and over 560 nurseries where you can buy them.*
www.rhs.org.uk

### Crocus

*Online supplier of plants and other garden related merchandise.*
www.crocus.co.uk

### Plant Heritage

*Charity running the National Plant Collection scheme helping to conserve groups of related plants. Over 660 national collection holders, including the National Trust. Check website for events and plant sales.*
www.nccpg.com

### Sarah Raven

*Seeds, bulbs, plants and garden lifestyle products with a focus on decorative plants and flowers.*
www.sarahraven.com

### Chiltern Seeds

*Huge and diverse range of around 4,000 different seeds, from vegetables to flowers.*
www.chilternseeds.co.uk

### Jekka's Herb Farm

*Organic herb nursery with over 650 varieties of culinary, aromatic, decorative and medicinal herbs. Online shop with occasional open days and events.*
www.jekkasherbfarm.com

### Heritage Seed Library

*Run by the charity Garden Organic to conserve rare varieties of vegetables.*
www.gardenorganic.org.uk

### David Austin Roses

*English rose specialists, over 900 varieties of old, shrub, species, climbing and modern roses.*
www.davidaustinroses.com

### Blackmoor Fruit Nursery

*Specialist mail order fruit nursery.*
www.blackmoor.co.uk

### Really Wild Flowers

*Online specialists in native British wild flower seeds, plug plants, bulb and hedgerow trees.*
www.reallywildflowers.co.uk

### Pictorial Meadows Seeds

*Founded by Professor Nigel Dunnett of the University of Sheffield who created the London 2012 Olympic Park annual meadows. Seed mixes of native and non-native hardy annuals designed for visual impact and to flower over long periods.*
www.pictorialmeadows.co.uk

### Topiary Organisation

*Website with information on topiary growers and suppliers.*
www.topiary.org.uk

There are also many specialist plant societies, including the Hardy Plant Society and the Cottage Garden Society who have useful websites if you are interested in finding out more about a specific range of plants.

# Hard landscaping and garden features

## Garden Furniture
*Gaze and Burvill National Trust collection of outdoor furniture.*
www.gazeburvill.com

## Lutyens Furniture and Lighting
*Official makers of Lutyens benches and a range of other outdoor furniture.*
www.lutyens-furniture.com

## Westminster Stone
*Paving and decorative stone, including traditional flagstones, including a National Trust collection.*
www.nationaltrustpaving.com

## Oak Leaf Gates
*Traditional and contemporary oak gate design.*
www.oakleafgates.co.uk

## Salvo
*Directory of suppliers of architectural salvage, including cast iron, bricks and stone. Also lists UK fairs and auctions.*
www.salvo.co.uk

## David Harber
*Traditional and contemporary sundials, water features and garden sculpture.*
www.davidharber.co.uk

## The Fountain Society
*Encourages the restoration and use of water features in gardens and has a useful website.*
www.fountainsoc.org.uk

## Turners Ornamental Leadwork
*Contemporary ornamental leadwork, cisterns and sculpture and also conservation of old lead.*
www.turners-lead-collection.co.uk

## Whichford Pottery
*Wide range of handmade clay flower pots. Events and sales at the pottery in Warwickshire or buy online.*
www.whichfordpottery.com

# index

**Pages in bold indicate photographs**

# picture credits

©Jacq Barber: 86, 87 top right, 90 right, 163 bottom.
©Blacker Design: p171.
©Peter Hall: p124–5, 136 left.
©Penny James: p169 bottom.
©David Harber: p148.
©Cara Lockhart Smith: p63.

©National Trust/Mike Calnan: p169 top; ©NT/Neil Cook: p138 middle; ©NT/Alexa Datta: p129 left; ©NT/Andy Eddy: p118; ©NT/Victoria Evans: p32, p41, 66 top and bottom, 75 top, 110, 111 top and bottom; ©NT/Penny Hammond: p166, 167 top; ©NT/Tina Hammond: pp60–61, 74 bottom; ©NT/Kaye Haworth: p72 left; ©NT/Tim Hemming: p103 top right, p130 bottom right, 131 top, p134 right; ©NT/Lou Horrod: p157 left; ©NT/Ian Hunt: p121 top; ©NT/Holly Jones: 113 bottom; ©NT/Averil Milligan: p119 top; ©NT/Chris Orton: p36, 42; ©NT/Alison Pringle: p65 middle and right; ©NT/Steve Spearing: p131 bottom; ©NT/Richard Todd: p88, 100 bottom right; ©NT/Paul Watson: p50, 58, 112, 113 top left and right, 143 bottom; ©NT/Woolbeding Garden: p115 bottom; ©NT/Ian Wright: p145 left.

©National Trust Images/John Blake: p138 top; ©NTI /Mark Bolton: p31 (clockwise, 3rd and 11th from top), 33 right, 40 right, 70–71, 73 top middle and bottom right, 83 left, 91 bottom, 97 bottom right, 100 top right, 108, 121 bottom left, 122 top and bottom right, 130 top right, 157 right bottom, 158, 159, 161 top right, 165 middle and bottom; ©NTI /Jonathan Buckley: p5, 11 top, 13 left, 14 left, 14 right, 16 top, 16 bottom, 17 bottom, 24, 25, 28–29, 34, 35 top left, 38, 46–47, 54, 55 bottom, 59 top left, 59 top right, 76, 78 left and right, 79 top right, 104 top, 121 bottom right, 126, 127 top middle and right and bottom, 133 top, 133 bottom right, 134 left, 137 top and bottom, 147 top left, 149 bottom right, 160, 162 left and right; ©NTI /Andrew Butler: p10 top, 12 left and right, 15 right, 17 middle, 26, 30, 31 (clockwise, 6th from top), 39 bottom, 55 top right, 56, 69 bottom right, 72 right, 82 top, 85 bottom right, 89 top left, 127 top left, 135 top and bottom, 136 right, 144 left and right, 146 left, 164 bottom, 168; ©NTI /Neil Campbell-Sharp: p44; ©NTI /Brian & Nina Chapple: p147 top right; ©NTI /Vera Collingwood: p52; ©NTI /Val Corbett: p31 (top), 51 top, 89 bottom middle, 116 top right; ©NTI /Joe Cornish: p17 top, 21 bottom, 87 bottom right; ©NTI /Stuart Cox: p51 bottom

right, 151 left top and bottom; ©NTI /Derek Croucher: p97 bottom left, 140–141; ©NTI /Dennis Davis: p109 right; ©NTI /Arnhel de Serra: p21 top, 31 (clockwise, 7th from top), 122 bottom left, 149 bottom left, 150; ©NTI/David Dixon: p59 top middle, 73 top middle and bottom middle, 85 bottom middle; ©NTI/James Dobson: p147 bottom; ©NTI /Rod Edwards: p103 bottom left, 104 bottom, 105 bottom right; ©NTI /Phil Evans: p157 right top; ©NTI /Simon Fraser: p62; ©NTI /Christopher Gallagher: p33 left, 96; ©NTI /Jonathan Gibson: p27 right; ©NTI /Dennis Gilbert: p84; ©NTI /John Hammond: p97 top right, 101 top; © NTI /Derek Harris: p156 right; ©NTI/Ross Hoddinott: p165 top; ©NTI/Angelo Hornak: p10 bottom; ©NTI/Jerry Harpur: p39 top, 146 right; ©NTI/Paul Harris: p43 right, 53 bottom, 69 bottom left, 73 bottom left, 87 bottom left, 109 left, 122 bottom middle, 132 left; ©NTI//Roger Hickman: p120 top; ©NTI/Ross Hoddinott: p161 bottom; ©NTI//Andrea Jones: p22, 31 (clockwise, 4th and 5th from top), 35 bottom right, 48 top, 88 bottom left, 103 top left, 166 bottom; ©NTI/NaturePL/David Kjaer: p142 bottom; ©NTI/Andrew Lawson: p19 bottom, 27 left, 37 bottom, 95 left, 98, 101 bottom right; ©NTI/David Levenson: p121 bottom middle, 123 top; ©NTI/ Anthony Lord: p37 top; ©NTI//Marianne Majerus: pp2–3; ©NTI//MMGI/Marianne Majerus: p98, 99 bottom left and right, 100 top left and middle, 100 bottom, 102 top right, 102 bottom left; ©NTI/Nick Meers: p18, 19 top, 69 top right, 142 top; ©NTI/John Millar: p85 top left, 87 top left, 92–93, 101 bottom left, 109 middle, 116 bottom right, 152–153, 164 top; ©NTI /John Miller: p64, 65 left, 145 right; ©NTI /Paul Mogford: p13 right, 156 left; ©NTI /Geoff Morgan: p128 bottom; ©NTI /Robert Morris: p11 bottom, 31 (clockwise, 2nd from top), 51 bottom left, 68, 80–81, 128 top,139; ©NTI /Clive Nichols: p45; ©NTI /Alan Novelli: p105 top right and bottom left; ©NTI /Stephen Robson: pp6–7, 15 left, 20, 22–23, 31 (clockwise, 8th, 9th, 10th and 12th from top), 35 top right and bottom left, 40 left, 43 left and middle, 48 bottom, 49, 57 top right and bottom, 59 bottom, 69 top left, 73 top left, 77, 79 top left, 79 bottom left and right, 83 right top and bottom, 85 bottom left, 89 top right and bottom, 90 left, 91 top, 97 top left, 100 bottom middle, 102 top left, 103 bottom right, 105 top left, 106–107, 114, 115 top, 116 top left and bottom left, 117 top and bottom left, 119 bottom, 120 bottom, 123 middle, 123 bottom, 129 right, 130 left, 138 bottom, 143 top, 149 top, 154,155,161 left top, 163 top; ©NTI/David Sellman: pp8–9, 132 right, 133 bottom left; ©NTI /William Shaw: p117 top left; ©NTI /Andreas von Einsiedel: p4; ©NTI /Charlie Waite: p55 top left, 57 top left and middle; ©NTI /Ian West: p82 bottom, 95 right, 102 top right, 145 middle, 151 right.

# acknowledgements

I am grateful to my friend and colleague Alison Dalby, who came up with the original concept for this book and has written the companion title *Design Ideas for your Home*. It has been an enjoyable journey working on these books together.

At the National Trust I would like to thank John Stachiewicz, Grant Berry and Chris Lacey for all their help. At Anova, my thanks to Cathy Gosling, Lucy Smith who has provided encouragement and advice at every stage and Lee-May Lim for her inspiring design.

Most of all, I am indebted to the many National Trust head gardeners, gardens consultants, gardens staff and volunteers who were so generous with their time and expertise. In particular, my thanks to Claire Abery, Val Anderson, Christine Brain, Neil Cook, Alexis Datta, Andy Eddy, Rachel Edwards, John Ellis, Mick Evans, Victoria Evans, Nick Fraser, Peter Hall, Penny Hammond, Tina Hammond, Nick

Haworth, Philippa Hodkinson, Jo Hooper, Andy Jesson, Averil Milligan, Andrew Mudge, Neil Porteous, Ned Price, Alison Pringle, Cat Saunders, Glyn Smith, Tommy Teagle, Richard Todd, Paul Underwood, Philip Whaites and Ian Wright.

Jonathan Buckley, Tim Hemming and Paul Watson have helped me enormously, providing many of the fabulous photographs in this book.

My gratitude to Siân Evans for her much valued advice, and to Patricia Hicks Harris, Kathy Drake, Belinda Crawley and Susana Stevens who have supported me throughout.

Last but not least, Mike Calnan, Head of Gardens at the National Trust, has cast a constructive critical eye at every stage and offered his unflagging support while this book was being written.